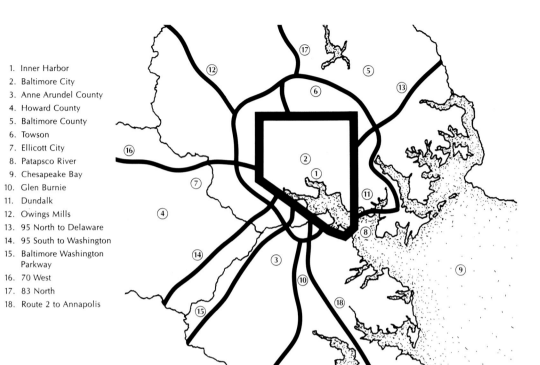

1. Inner Harbor
2. Baltimore City
3. Anne Arundel County
4. Howard County
5. Baltimore County
6. Towson
7. Ellicott City
8. Patapsco River
9. Chesapeake Bay
10. Glen Burnie
11. Dundalk
12. Owings Mills
13. 95 North to Delaware
14. 95 South to Washington
15. Baltimore Washington Parkway
16. 70 West
17. 83 North
18. Route 2 to Annapolis

CONTENTS

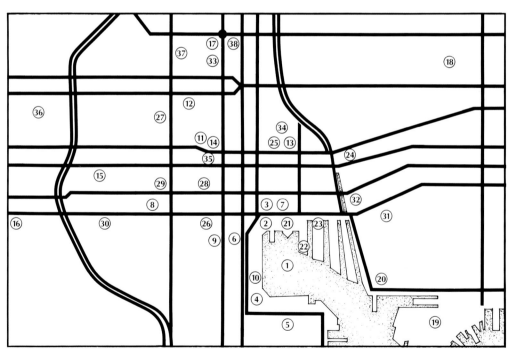

1. Inner Harbor
2. Harborplace
3. Gallery at Harborplace
4. Maryland Science Center
5. Federal Hill
6. Hyatt Regency Hotel
7. Stouffer Harborplace Hotel
8. Baltimore Marriott-Inner Harbor Hotel
9. Sheraton Inner Harbor Hotel
10. Harbor Court Hotel
11. Omni Inner Harbor Hotel
12. Peabody Court Hotel
13. War Memorial Plaza
14. Lord Baltimore Radisson Plaza
15. University of Maryland at Baltimore
16. B&O Railroad Museum
17. Washington Monument/Mount Vernon
18. Johns Hopkins Hospital
19. Fells Point
20. Little Italy
21. World Trade Center
22. National Aquarium
23. P.T. Flaggs
24. Shot Tower
25. City Hall
26. Baltimore Convention Center
27. Lexington Market
28. Baltimore Arena
29. Baltimore Arts Tower
30. Babe Ruth Birthplace and Baltimore Orioles Museum
31. Star Spangled Banner Flag House
32. Carroll Mansion
33. Walters Art Gallery
34. Peale Museum
35. Morris A. Mechanic Theatre
36. Edgar Allan Poe House
37. Maryland Historical Society
38. Peabody Conservatory

BALTIMORE A PORTRAIT

Robin Levin, Photographer

IMAGE   PUBLISHING,   LTD.

IMAGE PUBLISHING, LTD.

1411 Hollins Street/Union Square

301 • 566-1222   Baltimore, Maryland 21223   301 • 624-5253

CREDITS

Photography by Roger Miller
Design by David Miller
Text by Ron Pilling
Text edited by Margaretta H. Finn
Text coordinated by Sarah C. Carter
Typesetting and layouts by Delta Graphics, Inc.
Original color separations by DAI Nippon Printing Co., Ltd., Tokyo, Japan
Printing, new color separations, and binding by Everbest Printing Co., Ltd.,
    Hong Kong

INFORMATION

Library of Congress Catalog Card Number:
Original hardcover: 82-091142
Original softcover: 83-090131
Revised hardcover: 88-081951
Revised softcover: 88-081951

ISBN #: 0-911897-00-3 (1st. edition hardcover)
ISBN #: 0-911897-01-1 (1st. edition softcover)
ISBN #: 0-911897-14-3 (**revised hardcover**)
ISBN #: 0-911897-15-1 (**revised softcover**)

First Printing 1983, Second Printing 1984, Third Printing, 1985. Revised and Fourth Printing 1988, Fifth Printing 1990.
Printed in Hong Kong.

DEDICATION
RUTH DORA MILLER AND **CHARLES JOHN EDWARD MILLER**

I would like to dedicate this book to my parents for their love, friendship and patience. Thank you!

Roger Miller, 8-8-83

How can two people keep getting better?

Roger Miller, 7-7-88

SPECIAL THANKS

I would like to thank everyone who had a part in this project. I would especially like to thank the following:

A special thanks to all the people and businesses of Maryland. Without their hard work and dedication to making Maryland the great state it is, this book would not have been possible.

I would like to thank **Mayor Kurt L. Schmoke** for his assistance in writing the foreword to "Baltimore A Portrait."

For their efforts and belief in this project I would like to thank everyone at **NCNB of Maryland** particularly **Lee Boatwright, Mike Glump,** and **Gail Houser**. NCNB is truly a bank which believes in the people and the state of Maryland.

A very special thanks to **Wayne Chapell,** Executive Director of the Baltimore Convention Bureau, for his friendship, foresight and commitment to new ideas to promote both Baltimore and Maryland.

I would like to thank my dedicated staff for putting up with some of the pressures we have dealt with in creating our books. Without the efforts and devotion of **Sarah C. Carter** and **Margaretta H. Finn** this book would not exist.

Roger Miller

ORDERS

For direct orders please call or write for specific cost and postage and handling to the above address. Discounts available for stores and institutions, minimum orders required.

BALTIMORE A PORTRAIT

Photography By Roger Miller
Foreword by Kurt L. Schmoke, Mayor

Text by Ron Pilling

Design, Editing By David Miller

FOREWORD

By Kurt L. Schmoke, Mayor

One of the most common reactions of first-time visitors to Baltimore is, "This is Baltimore?"
Yes, this is Baltimore.

For the people and families who have grown up in Baltimore (many of whom trace their Baltimore roots back for generations), and for the newly arrived as well, Baltimore is a treasure filled city, rich in history, architecture, music, food, waterfront beauty, literature, science and identity.

It's this last quality – identity – that makes Baltimore particularly special. Baltimore is a city with character. It is the home or birthplace of Justice Thurgood Marshall, Anne Tyler, Eubie Blake and John Waters, among other distinguished Americans. Baltimore's cultural, linguistic and historical flavor sets it apart, and makes it a place you want to come home to.

The people of Baltimore are tremendously proud of the changes that have taken place here in the last 15 years – many of which are showcased in this book. But even without the Inner Harbor, the Gallery and the other gleaming new office buildings, Baltimore would still be the place we would want to raise our children. That is because beyond the Harbor, the Washington Monument and the homes of H.L. Mencken, Babe Ruth, and Edgar Allan Poe, are the homes and neighborhoods of the people of Baltimore. And it's there that Baltimore's identity comes to life.

Whether you visit Hampstead Hill in East Baltimore, Union Square in West Baltimore, Roland Park, Federal Hill, Windsor Hills, Charles Village, Highlandtown, Forest Park or any of Baltimore's other proud neighborhoods, you will find the beauty and energy of Baltimore. Each of these communities has a color, shape and texture all its own, and together they give Baltimore its special signature – as a place where families can grow and prosper, and business and visitors are always welcome.

Making Baltimore a national attraction – which resulted from the public and private sectors working together – has stimulated neighborhood preservation and revitalization efforts. These efforts are being led by partnerships composed of business, community and religious

organizations, and government. Homes are being restored, and whole neighborhoods – including commercial districts – are being rebuilt.

Also located in Baltimore are internationally renowned hospitals, museums, universities, and industrial research centers. Scholarship, creativity and scientific discovery have long flourished in Baltimore and will continue to do so.

There is a consensus in Baltimore that this City – which at one time had been nearly written off as an example of industrial and urban decay – should serve as a model for what can be accomplished by any proud and hardworking community.

Baltimore always had hope and promise, and now we have much to show for it. Since the first edition of Roger Miller's "Baltimore A Portrait," the Baltimore skyline has changed significantly. The Walters Art Gallery has been renovated, an IMAX theater has been added to the Maryland Science Center. Old factories have been converted into comfortable downtown living spaces for thousands of people, and modern movie and entertainment complexes have been built or are under construction.

As for the future, a new baseball stadium will be built at Camden Yards and a marine mammal exhibit will soon be added to the National Aquarium. And that is only the beginning. With their creative drive and cooperative spirit, the people of Baltimore will continue to remake this City without ever relinquishing its historic character.

I invite you to look through the pages of this book. Go slowly and enjoy the view. Baltimore is wonderful blend of old and new, and Roger Miller has beautifully captured the essence of both.

Baltimore, you will quickly discover, is a wonderful place to live.

Kurt L. Schmoke

Kurt L. Schmoke, Mayor

INTRODUCTION

On a warm spring morning a soldier leans against a high wooden piling, watching out across the Baltimore harbor through a forest of tall masts, a web of tarred rigging. He wears the uniform of a foot soldier of the First Maryland Regiment, indirectly under the command of General George Washington. His musket leans against one leg, his leather haversack hangs loosely from the post.

But wait, this is not Revolutionary War Baltimore. It is the twentieth century, and the infantryman will be marching in a parade from East Baltimore's Fells Point to Federal Hill, overlooking the Inner Harbor. The event commemorates the 200th anniversary of the signing of the Constitution by the State of Maryland. Like the celebration of two centuries earlier, Baltimoreans portraying the trades of the waning 1700's – shipwrights, blacksmiths, apothecaries and more – will parade through Baltimore streets praising the document wrought by Marylanders and others in Philadelphia. The only difference is that these modern Baltimoreans merely dress the part.

For this is Baltimore, Maryland, a city proud of its three hundred years of progress but a city which, fortunately, refuses to let go of the past.

When the returning soldiers from the Revolutionary War laid aside their weapons and went back to the shipyards, the brickworks, the breweries and the docks along the city's Patapsco River, they were unknowingly laying the foundations for a city which, by the time of the Constitutional Bicentennial, would be the focal point for over a million Marylanders. Baltimore has become the region's banking and financial headquarters, a major center of manufacturing, and a cornerstone in the transportation industry of the entire East Coast.

It all began at this spot where the accountant costumed as an eighteenth century soldier scans the modern Inner Harbor. The earliest known picture of the city, depicting Baltimore in 1752, shows a small but thriving town. A cluster of a dozen or so buildings; simple box-like houses, a tavern or two, a church and several small businesses dot the hillside overlooking the harbor. Baltimore Town was dwarfed by Jonestown and Fells Point to the east, both major centers of trade and shipbuilding. The three would become the nucleus of the modern city of Baltimore.

By the Revolutionary War there were nearly six hundred houses dominating the harborscape. Economic growth, especially along the creek valleys to the north, was creating a class of landed gentry and merchants that had a decided stake in the trading interests that operated along the narrow alleys and wooden wharves of the Patapsco basin. Two commodities – iron and wheat – drove the local economy during its important early years. The streams that ran into Baltimore from the hills to the north and west provided power for the water-driven mills that threshed the grain and hammered the iron bars that eventually made their way to the harbor. Many early attempts to establish towns in the Chesapeake Bay watershed had failed, but Baltimore, with its natural harbor, its rich resources and its proximity to the productive lands nearby, became the state's major market center by the close of the Revolution.

In 1776, John Adams visited Baltimore while serving in the Continental Congress. Its merchants were prosperous and its businesses flourishing, and the Massachusetts congressman admired the revolutionary spirit of the people. Perhaps it was our war for independence that set Baltimore squarely on the road to greatness. The war generated tremendous demand for the town's two most important products, iron and wheat, allowing Baltimore families to participate actively in the struggle for freedom from England. Being a shipbuilding center, Baltimore contributed 250 privateers (little more than pirates), but the nucleus of the fledgling American Navy) to the fight. The growth of manufacturing helped the city break from the tobacco-farming tradition. The city opened its arms to immigrants from Ireland and Germany, Scotland and France, and each new group contributed to Baltimore's rapid expansion.

By the time Jonestown, Fells Point, and Baltimore Town were incorporated into one city the economic direction had long been decided. There was much rivalry between the three villages that coalesced into a mercantile power, differences that mark the city and give it much of its character to this day. In 1796, when Baltimore was officially incorporated, the residents thought of their home not as a village, but as a city, and Baltimore had become an important cog in the financial and trade machinery of the western world.

A post-Revolution generation took the reins of progress, and the city entered a period of rapid expansion that would continue unabated in spite of the British bombardment of Baltimore's Fort McHenry in 1814. Financial institutions were created to meet the tremendous demand for banking and brokerage services. A host of related trades sprang up in the closing years of the 1700's. There were six newspapers on the streets by 1799, the number of printers and publishers quadrupled, and an entire community of craftsmen – shipfitters, brewers, bakers, soap boilers, leatherworkers, and coopers – sprang up as a direct result of commercial growth.

So it was that Baltimore found herself in an enviable position when the War of 1812 broke out. She sent hundreds of privateers in the feared "Baltimore Clippers," low-slung sailboats built for speed as well as for cargo, against the powerful British fleet. In September, 1814, British forces under General Robert Ross sailed up the Chesapeake to crush the "nest of pirates." Meeting defeat at the hands of the Baltimore militia near North Point, and repulsed after a 24-hour bombardment of Fort McHenry at the mouth of the harbor, the invaders sailed away.

It was during the bombardment that Francis Scott Key, a local lawyer who observed the merciless cannonading from the decks of a British frigate, was inspired to pen what would become the National Anthem. Within days the poem became a rallying cry, and Baltimoreans were overnight heroes.

Within three months the war was over and Baltimore could return its attention to economic growth. Peace brought prosperity, the clipper ships returned to trade, and steam power carried the city into a new industrial era. In the first forty years of the 1800's the population expanded from about twenty-five thousand to over a hundred thousand. New roads connected Baltimore with cities to the west, canals were built to move goods to the growing region along the Ohio River, and the railroad was born. In 1830, the Baltimore and Ohio Railroad started the first

commercial rail service in the country, and Baltimore became the first city of rail travel. Dominance in railroading would sustain the unheralded growth for over seventy years.

It was the city's fortunate location which fostered this expansion. Baltimore was the closest port city to Pittsburgh, cutting out over a hundred miles of land transportation compared to either Philadelphia or Alexandria. The birth of the railroad here strenghtened Baltimore's commercial dominance and spurred the city's continued growth.

On the eve of the Civil War, Baltimore found itself a city divided. Though most of its trade was with the North, there was a strong attachment to the Confederate states. Landed gentry whose plantations surrounded Baltimore still owned slaves. While some Baltimoreans supported Lincoln in the election of 1861, others openly espoused secession. On April 19 the first blood of the war was shed on Baltimore streets when troops of the Sixth Massachusetts Regiment were attacked by a Baltimore mob. Throughout the rest of the war the city was virtually captive, guarded by 1500 federal troops armed with heavy cannon commanding a threatening position from Federal Hill.

The city remained relatively unscathed during the war and emerged to continue its earlier mercantile domination of the Mid-Atlantic region. The decades between the Civila War and World War I saw both economic and social change. Horse car lines, and later trolleys, enabled Baltimoreans to move away from the harbor. Public education offered new opportunities to a generation of Baltimoreans, and men who had made huge fortunes here gave some of their wealth back to a grateful population.

In 1866, philanthropist George Peabody dedicated the Peabody Institute, a world-respected center of musical education. Enoch Pratt's generous donation to the city of Baltimore resulted in the opening of the Enoch Pratt Library in 1886. Johns Hopkins gave much of his multi-million dollar estate for the creation of Johns Hopkins Hospital and University. Merchant Moses Sheppard created what would become the Sheppard and Enoch Pratt Hospital. Dozens of other moneyed Baltimoreans did the same, founding schools, hospitals, and museums. After a century of continual growth, Baltimore was beginning to become a well-rounded city, offering opportunities that would enrich the lives of many of its residents.

The period between the Civil War and World War I saw the greatest influx of immigrants to Baltimore in its entire history. Most came from Germany and Ireland, though Czechs, Poles, Jews, Lithuanians and others from Eastern Europe also passed through the Locust Point reception center. Ethnic neighborhoods, like Little Italy just east of the Inner Harbor, the Greek neighborhood along Eastern Avenue, Little Lithuania scattered around Lithuanian Hall on Hollins Street, and the Polish enclave in Fells Point near St. Stanislaus Church, remain as testament to the courage and industry of the new Americans.

While people were on their way to church, on February 7, 1904, an event which would both mark the opening of the new century and contribute to changing the face of the city for decades was smoldering in the dry goods warehouse of the John F. Hurst Company on Hopkins Place. The Great Baltimore Fire destroyed over a thousand commercial buildings and scorched one hundred and forty acres. By the time the flames reached Jones Falls early Monday morning, fire companies from as far away as Philadelphia had rushed to the scene by special train to assist the Baltimore firefighters.

The city quickly went on to rebuild. The financial center, where most of the damage had occurred, moved ahead with scarcely a pause. Though many local insurance companies were bankrupted by ensuing claims, the fire represented little more than a pause in Baltimore's economic progress.

Baltimoreans contributed to the war efforts in both World Wars by sending their sons to fight and by redoubling manufacturing efforts to meet the nation's requirements for armaments. Seemingly Baltimore was destined to move into the second half of the twentieth century with its historic, economic and social power intact.

But like all older, manufacturing-based American cities, Baltimore was to experience both economic and social change beyond anything in her three hundred year history. By 1950 a third of the population lived in poverty and local leadership had to face the problems. Black leaders began to move into elective offices in Baltimore much earlier than in any other southern city, contributing to the city's relatively early advances toward racial and social equality.

In 1961, the groundbreaking for One Charles Center marked the beginning of a major downtown renewal effort that shifted into high gear in the 1970's and 1980's. An unheralded partnership between local government and private investment began to change the face of the city.

The election of William Donald Schaefer to the mayoralty in 1971 added a powerful catalyst to the process. Schaefer, a combination of unabashed cheerleader for the city, determined negotiator and dealmaker, and publicist extraordinaire, had a vision for Baltimore that to most seemed impossibly progressive. Even Baltimoreans themselves, especially those who had fled the city for the suburbs during the fifties and sixties, thought that Schaefer was a dreamer.

That he was, but his dreams quickly began to come true. He saw in Baltimore a city whose unique character could attract millions of visitors each year, visitors who would spend their money along the harbor's edge and in doing so create jobs and prosperity. When Harborplace opened in 1980 no one could argue about the mayor's success or about the new face of a town that newspapers across the country had begun to call "Charm City".

As energetic new city homeowners begin to restore the ancient brick rowhouses that line Baltimore streets, entire neighborhoods take on a new pride and a new charisma. It seems that a new restaurant opens in Baltimore every week or so and major hotel chains fight for land near the Inner Harbor. Conventioneers book city facilities years in advance. With a new respect for itself, Baltimore is looking forward to the twenty-first century, confident that the enthusiasm and industry of her residents will assure her continued growth.

INNER HARBOR

If ever a city could boast that in returning to its roots it found the resources it needed to face an uncertain future, Baltimore is that city. For in Baltimore, the focus of the city fathers has returned time and time again to the harbor. The most recent return, however – the one that capitalized the words "Inner Harbor" – marked both a dramatic change in the traditional role of the waterfront in Baltimore as well as a direction for the city for decades to come.

Baltimore's Inner Harbor is the jewel in the crown of the city's renaissance. Its success is symbolic of the vision of a handful of business and government leaders who saw in their hometown more than just a blue-collar working city. The millions who visit the Inner Harbor each year attest to the wisdom of that vision, and the harbor's pavilions, shops and restaurants are usually the first stops for out-of-towners.

Years after its opening, the National Aquarium still draws huge crowds that line up daily outside the glass pavilion on Pier 3. A stop for lunch at Harborplace, perhaps a crab cake or half-a-dozen Chincoteague oysters, is a must on the day's schedule. There's exclusive shopping at The Gallery, paddleboats, the spectacular IMAX movie theatre in the Maryland Science Center, and dozens of other attractions in the panorama tightly woven around the Patapsco basin.

Yet just thirty years ago the harbor was the last place a native would want to take his uncle and aunt from Tulsa for a day's enjoyment. Rotting piers lined the Light Street side of the harbor. There was little commercial shipping, though the odd, rust-streaked tramp freighter would pull up from time to time. If there was any nighttime action at all, it was probably at the City Morgue, just a block or two from the present Harborplace.

This is the same harbor which, in the 1752 drawing of Baltimore Town, was a pastoral village. Several fishermen pull their nets in the shadow of Federal Hill while a single sloop rides at anchor on what would become the Light Street bulkhead. A couple dozen buildings rise on the gentle slope, and plowed fields cover the site of today's Pier 6 Harborlights Pavilion.

It was the protected Patapsco Basin which drew people here in the first place, and the basin would be the focal point of the town well into the twentieth century. Early photographs show an observation tower atop Federal Hill, whose red clay flanks drop precipitously to the water. Tall-masted boats line all three banks. The wharves along Light and Pratt Streets teem with horse-drawn wagons filled with all imaginable cargoes. The lines of wagons often extended for blocks in every direction.

Along Light Street stood the offices and wharves of companies that offered steamboat service for both passengers and cargo up and down the Chesapeake. Their destinations – Richmond, Petersburg, Raleigh and Lynchburg – were painted in gilt letters along their bracketed rooflines. Women with parasols and men in stovepipe hats fought their way past the drovers to claim a berth.

After over two centuries of productive commercial activities, the basin in the 1950's had sunk to its lowest level. Shipping had moved to the outer harbor and the buildings that surrounded the Basin were abandoned, crumbling. What had been the city's gate to the world was an embarrassing eyesore.

Under the leadership of Mayor William Donald Schaefer, however, the focus of city development looked once again to the Inner Harbor. The mayor proposed a broad, energetic development plan that would make the old Basin the centerpiece of the new Baltimore. In a new spirit of cooperation, government learned to work with developers whose contributions could match the mayor's vision. By September 1979, when ground was broken for Harborplace, that dream was well on its way to reality.

Developer James Rouse's Harborplace pavilions have become the anchor in an exciting panorama of new buildings, or new uses for old buildings. One of the green-roofed Harborplace buildings houses shops and restaurants, and the other is a festival of small food vendors, restaurants and tiny shops. Chesapeake Bay fare – crabs, clams, corn-on-the-cob, fish and fried chicken – are staples here, complemented by a mouth-watering vista of international foods. Shops feature everything from local crafts and souvenirs to high fashion.

Anchored in the shelter of Harborplace is the *U.S.F. Constellation*, the first ship launched by the United States Navy in 1797, built in nearby Harris Creek just a mile or so from its present berth. The *Constellation* has been recently restored and dramatizes shipboard life from the early days of the country.

The *Constellation* is the focal point for a growing regatta of historic boats and ships as well as private pleasure craft. During summer months, the Chesapeake Bay Skipjack *Minnie V* sails daily from the Inner Harbor for waterfront tours (in the winter, she still dredges for oysters). The *Lady Maryland*, a reproduction Pungy Schooner, provides a classroom-on-the-water for Baltimore schoolchildren.

Baltimore's "floating ambassador," the *Pride of Baltimore II*, also calls the Inner Harbor its home port. The *Pride II*, begun in 1987 after a tragic storm took her namesake, will sail around the globe spreading the good news about Baltimore. A reproduction of the famous Baltimore Clippers, the *Pride II* is low and fast, beautiful under sail.

Among the first new buildings on the Inner Harbor was the Maryland Science Center, home of the Maryland Academy of Sciences, the oldest scientific academy in the nation. This contemporary building at the harbor's southwest corner houses the Davis Planetarium and displays on everything from computers to Chesapeake Bay ecology. Its newest addition is the IMAX movie theatre, featuring a tall, wrap-around screen that truly brings its presentations into three-dimensional life.

The harbor's most popular attraction has always been the National Aquarium. A dynamic building, with a rain forest housed in a glass pyramid which overlooks the Constellation's berth, the aquarium is home to 6000 specimens – fish, reptiles, tropical plants, and more. Animals and plants are displayed in life-like artificial environments, including the tropical rain forest, a shark tank, and an Atlantic coral reef.

So in just several decades, the basin has become the Inner Harbor. There is more, like the Top of the World, an observation deck atop the World Trade Center featuring displays of harbor history, the Pier 6 concert pavilion, and The Gallery, a sparkling new multi-level shopping mall attached to the Stouffer Harborplace Hotel. Baltimoreans and out-of-town guests alike flock to the new Inner Harbor, just as Baltimoreans have returned to the harbor year after year, century after century.

HARBORPLACE

If any single project could be said to have been the catalyst for the Baltimore renaissance of the 1970's and 1980's, it would have to be Harborplace. Costing an estimated $20 million, the project has more than met the expectations of its creators, former Mayor William Donald Schaefer and developer James Rouse.

HARBORPLACE

Two glass-enclosed pavillions house over 140 shops, restaurants, and informal eateries in Harborplace. One pavilion is a year-round diner's festival, with stalls serving everything from raw oysters to enchiladas. In the other pavilion, fashionable boutiques, gift shops, galleries, and fine restaurants vie for the visitor's attention.

THE GALLERY

A stunning four-story concoction of shopping and dining, The Gallery is Baltimore's newest attraction. The Stouffer Harborplace Hotel anchors one end of the building, while the other is filled with shops and restaurants surrounding a garden-like plaza.

The National Aquarium

Without water
there would be no...

THE NATIONAL AQUARIUM

Along Pier 3 just a block from Harborplace is the National Aquarium, the most technologically advanced facility of its kind in the nation. Six hundred species of birds, fish, and mammals call the glass-roofed building home. Visitors enjoy viewing the aquarium's inhabitants in startlingly realistic settings, duplicating a wide range of environments from a mountain stream to the famous rain forest that tops the building.

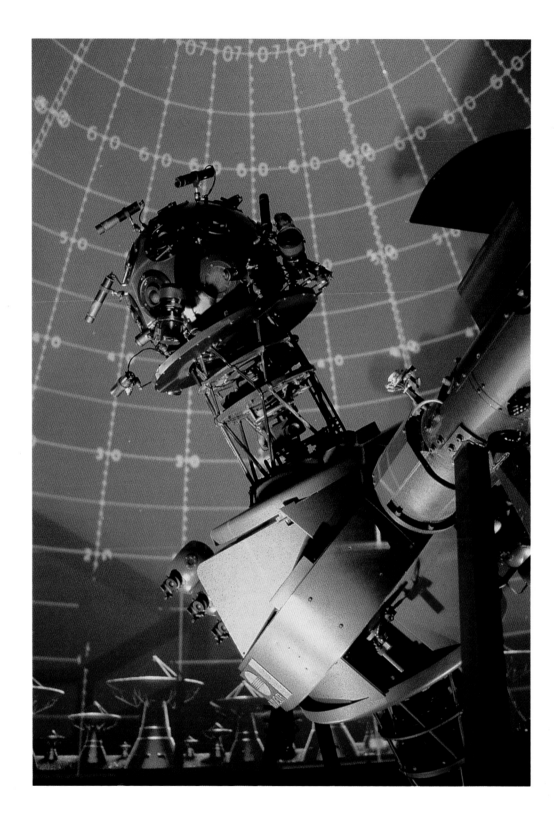

MARYLAND SCIENCE CENTER

The Maryland Academy of Sciences is the oldest organization in the country devoted to the study of science, and the Maryland Science Center is its home. Included are exhibits on evolution and the geology of the Chesapeake Bay, the Davis Planetarium, and the heart-stopping IMAX movie theatre.

WORLD TRADE CENTER

The world's tallest five-sided building, the World Trade Center was designed by world-famous architect I.M. Pei. The World Trade Center was begun in 1968, and is the informal headquarters of international trade and shipping for the Mid-Atlantic region. Atop the harborside tower is Top of the World, an observation room that provides a panoramic view of the city.

PIER 6 CONCERT PAVILION

    A modernistic canvas roof covers this 2000-seat pavilion that is home to the Harborlights Music Festival. Throughout the warm months of summer all types of music from rhythm and blues to Gershwin, from Peter, Paul and Mary to the Preservation Hall Jazz band, bursts forth from the huge tent across the harbor.

THE MARITIME INNER HARBOR

Recalling Baltimore's great seafaring heritage, pleasure boats share the modern harbor with several historic vessels. The USF Constellation, first ship of the United States Navy, is the harbor's floating centerpiece. Paddleboats dot the water as visitors and locals enjoy the scenery from afloat. Several cruise boats, including the *Lady Maryland* and the Chesapeake Skipjack *Minnie V* make daily cruises to Fort McHenry and beyond.

PRIDE OF BALTIMORE II

Among Baltimore's most important contributions to the nation's early history was the role her ships played in the fledgling Navy during both wars against England. The *Pride of Baltimore II* is a replica of a Baltimore schooner typical of the era, and serves as the city's floating ambassador around the world.

U.S. FRIGATE CONSTELLATION
In 1797, the *Constellation* was launched in a creek not far from her current Inner Harbor berth. She is the oldest warship afloat, and saw action for a century and a half before retiring at the close of World War II.

John Eager Howard Room at The Hotel Belvedere

HOTEL BELVEDERE

The Belvedere was the tallest building in Baltimore when it opened in 1903. Much has changed since then, but the Belvedere remains the same. As exemplified by the John Eager Howard Room, the Belvedere still shines with the grace, style, and charm of a gentler century. Guests may also sample the menu at the Owl Bar, a turn-of-the-century pub, or enjoy the view from the 13th floor, a contemporary lounge that features live jazz.

ENTERTAINMENT & RECREATION

Perhaps the dilemma of the seventh inning stretch at Baltimore's Memorial Stadium best exemplifies Baltimoreans' approach to having fun. No one can seem to decide on the music to broadcast over the loudspeaker while the fans are stretching for their beloved Orioles. Should it be the Beatles or John Denver's "Thank God I'm a Country Boy"? Fans love their big-city team, but many are in fact country people at heart. Baltimore natives just can't decide what they like best, so they do everything.

A summer weekend may include a fine French dinner at one of the many excellent hotel dining rooms scattered around the Inner Harbor, followed by a long night partying to country and western or old-time rock and roll in Fells Point. Maybe it's the spaghetti and ravioli dinner at St. Leo's in Little Italy and an evening on board one of the harbor cruise boats that will highlight a Sunday schedule. If the Orioles, the Blast, or the Skipjacks are in town, it's a sure bet that plenty of locals will be on hand to cheer. Of course, for many there's no better way to spend the afternoon than bent over a newspaper-covered table heaped with steaming, spicy, hard crabs, a wooden mallet in one's hand and a pitcher of beer at one's elbow.

Like everything else here, leisure is changing dramatically while somehow remaining the same. The opening of Harborplace brought a cosmopolitan air to a city which heretofore was pretty much a working-class town. Twenty years ago Baltimore was strictly a steak-and-seafood city, with a handful of ethnic eateries. Now one can find fine dining from all corners of the globe, for it seems as if an exciting new restaurant throws open its doors every week. The surprise is that the natives, long considered stuck in their ways, are trying all these new things and liking them.

The same can be said for other forms of leisure besides eating, although eating is still probably the favorite pastime in this city which Oliver Wendell Holmes once called the "gastronomic center of the universe." Pleasure boats flock to the Inner Harbor, sails fluttering on a horizon that not long ago was filled with little more than tugs and rusty old steamers. Retailing has changed since the days when the only place to shop was the four department stores at the corner of Howard and Lexington. Today, shops fill city streets and downtown plazas with designer fashions and safari gear, the newest electronic gadgetry, and crafts from as far away as the South Pacific.

Once, Baltimoreans went out of their way to avoid downtown, but now they swarm here year-round. When the weather is warm this is especially true, for the Inner Harbor and parks near it become a summer-long festival. Ethnic festivals fill calendars from May until the kids go back to school. Artscape, a celebration of Baltimore's role in the contemporary art scene, takes over the streets around The Maryland Institute for a weekend in July. The season is capped off with the Baltimore City Fair, a potpourri of games, rides, neighborhood and community displays, and, of course, food.

Baltimore's many parks are frequently the scene of smaller celebrations of city living. It's difficult to find a neighborhood in the city that doesn't boast at least a handkerchief-sized patch of greenery, and the city is blessed with many larger parks. Many are the endowments of wealthy Baltimoreans who left their estates to be used as public parks. Indeed, the estate names remain in many cases: Druid Hill, Clifton, and Montebello.

Druid Hill Park is the city's largest, on several hundred acres in northwest Baltimore. The park has extensive groves of trees and lawns, a bandstand, a lake, and the Baltimore Zoo. The Zoo has undergone a major renovation and modernization, and now visitors can enjoy the zoo's animals in settings similar to their natural habitats.

Patterson Park is the heart of East Baltimore's communities. Its pagoda stands on the hill where the British were repulsed in 1814. Today, Patterson Park has acres of lawns, a lake, and a swimming pool, together with baseball diamonds and athletic fields. In the summer the nearby neighborhood of Butcher's Hill sponsors a series of outdoor concerts that draw Baltimoreans from all across town for an evening picnic and everything musical from the Baltimore Symphony to ethnic dancing.

As visitors and Baltimoreans alike returned in droves to the city in the 1970's, the demand for new products, new pursuits, and new hotels grew. When the Baltimore Convention Center greeted its first guests in 1979 there were scarcely enough rooms available in town to house a convention of midget basketball stars. But within five or six years there were several thousand new rooms within an easy walk of the waterfront. The venerable Lord Baltimore was given a complete renovation to join the ranks of the glass-fronted Hyatt Regency, the Stouffer Harborplace Hotel, and the elegant Harbor Court. Other Baltimore establishments, including the world-famous Belvedere, were spruced up, and historic buildings were converted to hotels and guest houses.

So if a visitor's preference is an ultra-modern suite, he can choose the Marriott, the Omni, or the Sheraton. Maybe the intimacy of a guest house or a bed-and-breakfast inn is the choice. In that case, there's the Shirley House in Mount Vernon or the Admiral Fell Inn at the foot of Broadway in Fells Point.

Baltimore restaurants have come a long way from the fifties, when the typical fare was little more than steaks and chops, with the odd seafood entree thrown in. In Harborplace alone there are half-a-dozen restaurants featuring menus from the Orient, France, East India, and of course, the Maryland Eastern Shore.

But any guest who knows anything about Baltimore usually wants to try steamed crabs. The red-hot crustaceans have become the town's chief edible ambassador. H.L. Mencken wrote of the surprise of his New York friends when, upon arriving at his Hollins Street home for a "feast," they were led to the basement where a long table was covered with yesterday's *Sunpapers* and a bushel of steaming "jimmies" (large, heavy, male blue crabs).

After sundown the city takes on a different personality. The taverns of Fells Point feature hundreds of different varieties of beer and almost as many types of music. From country tunes at Ledbetter's to rock at On Broadway, music pulses into the narrow streets and alleys. In centuries past, Fells Point was the first dry land onto which visiting sailors stepped. The sailors are mostly gone but Fells Point remains the same.

There's no shortage of things to occupy one's time in this town. The trick, for someone here for but a short time, is to decide what to do. Be advised not to ask the advice of a Baltimorean, however. Locals can't even decide what kind of music they like during the ballgame.

HYATT REGENCY HOTEL

The Hyatt Regency benefits from a splendid location overlooking the Inner Harbor, and is connected by walkways to the Convention Center, Harborplace shops, and downtown offices. Berry & Elliots, a rooftop restaurant and lounge, offers one of Baltimore's most spectacular vantage points. The Hyatt Regency also boasts an outdoor pool, tennis courts, and a health club. A six story atrium softened by a waterfall and lush greenery set the tone for the Hyatt's atmosphere of casual elegance.

BALTIMORE MARRIOTT – INNER HARBOR HOTEL

The Baltimore Marriott-Inner Harbor Hotel welcomes guests with 352 well-appointed rooms, including 12 elegant suites. The hotel offers 12 meeting rooms, including the 6,264 foot Grand Ballroom. The Promenade Sea Grill Restaurant specializes in local seafood favorites, and songs from the 50's and 60's set the mood in Illusions Lounge. The Marriott also provides a complete health facility, including an indoor pool, whirlpool, and sauna.

PEABODY COURT HOTEL

Located in Mount Vernon, the Peabody Court, Baltimore's only member of Leading Hotels of The World, offers travelers an elegant, gracious alternative to the Inner Harbor. From the rooftop Conservatory Restaurant to the more informal Peabody's – An American Brasserie, the magnificent decor and attentive staff blend to offer a first class experience.

SHERATON INNER HARBOR HOTEL

One of Baltimore's leading business hotels is the Sheraton Inner Harbor. Located downtown at 300 South Charles Street, the Sheraton is connected by a skywalk to the adjacent Baltimore Convention Center, and is a block away from Harborplace. The hotel features 339 spacious guest rooms, many offering harborviews, a night club, indoor health facilities, and a seafood restaurant which offers excellent breakfast and luncheon buffets.

STOUFFER HARBORPLACE HOTEL

Enclosed in blue-green glass, the Stouffer Harborplace is a striking addition to the Baltimore skyline. With 622 guest rooms, including 60 suites and a 90-room club floor, the Stouffer is one of Baltimore's largest hotels. The hotel also features a health club, indoor pool, and rooftop garden. But its most unusual feature is its location: the Stouffer opens directly into The Gallery, the Harbor's newest mall, merging with it effortlessly to create a unique getaway only steps from the waterfront.

HARBOR COURT HOTEL

Elegantly beautiful Hampton's, the Harbor Court's gourmet restaurant, has been rated the "finest restaurant in Baltimore" by the *Baltimore Sun*. That same sense of style is evident throughout the hotel, in the Cafe Brighton, with its lemon silk walls, and in 203 exquisitely decorated suites. The Harbor Court also offers an indoor pool, a racquetball court, and a rooftop croquet court and tennis court.

OMNI INTERNATIONAL HOTEL

The twin-towered Omni Inner Harbor is Maryland's largest hotel and corporate conference center. Newly renovated with more than 700 guest rooms and 38,000 square feet of meeting space, the Omni features Jacqueline, an exciting European bistro with American specialties, complimentary Inner Harbor shuttle service for all guests, and 45 Omni Club guest rooms with a private lounge.

The Brass Elephant

The Prime Rib

Jacqueline Cafe & Bistro, Etc.

THE BRASS ELEPHANT, PRIME RIB, JACQUELINE CAFE & BISTRO, ETC.

Northern Italian cuisine is offered in an atmosphere of elegance at the Brass Elephant, a restored 1881 townhouse. The richly detailed decor of the Brass Elephant reflects a seldom seen era of opulence in Baltimore architecture. Since 1965, restaurant aficionados have called the Prime Rib Baltimore's only New York-style restaurant. If plush surroundings coupled with fine American cuisine are typical of a Manhattan eatery, then the Prime Rib fits the name.

Jacqueline, in the Omni Inner Harbor Hotel, combines the charm of a European bistro with American specialties and Chesapeake seafood. A popular breakfast and lunch choice of downtown executives, Jacqueline is also the perfect spot for dinner before or after the theatre. The restaurant features nightly entertainment with cabaret performances on the weekend.

Velleggia's

Tio Pepe

Tio Pepe

VELLEGIA'S

Vellegia's is the oldest family-owned restaurant in Little Italy, a neighborhood with dozens of Italian dining rooms. Since it opened in the 1930's as Enrico's Friendly Tavern, Vellegia's has been a Baltimore landmark.

TIO PEPE

This Spanish restaurant in a Franklin Street basement is a perennial Baltimore favorite. Whitewashed walls and superb service make Tio Pepe an ideal place for a romantic evening.

Lexington Market

Haussner's

Culinary Arts Institute

CULINARY ARTS INSTITUTE, LEXINGTON MARKET

Baltimore's International Culinary Arts Institute got its start training food service professionals in 1972. The school doubles as a restaurant where students sharpen their skills as chefs and servers, and the school's gourmet grocery is open to the public. The traditions of Lexington Market span two centuries. Dozens of individual stalls sell fresh meats, produce, seafood, and poultry, and other vendors offer a huge variety of prepared foods.

HAUSSNER'S

As much a local institution as a restaurant, Haussner's has greeted diners at its Highlandtown location since 1926. The menu is extensive, featuring everything from crab cakes to sauerbraten to what's reputed to be the best strawberry pie on the East Coast.

BALTIMORE CONVENTION CENTER

Since it opened in the summer of 1979, the Baltimore Convention Center's schedule has been filled with trade shows and national gatherings. The center hosts the region's largest annual arts and crafts show and antiques extravaganzas, as well as business and professional conventions for everyone from square dancers to clergy. Demand for the Convention Center's facilities resulted in construction of the adjacent Festival Hall. Dramatic architecture and a flexible layout make the Convention Center unique among large halls.

DRUID HILL PARK, HOME OF THE BALTIMORE ZOO

Nearly 100 animals live on 150 wooded acres at the Baltimore Zoo in Druid Hill Park. Open year round, the Zoo offers visitors an opportunity to see many animals in their natural settings: Masai lions and giraffes in a predator-prey, open-air exhibit, numerous endangered species that are being protected and sometimes bred, and the largest colony of black-footed penguins in the country. A focal point of the Zoo is the restored mansion that serves as administrative headquarters. The old Boat Lake is home to more than eighteen species of waterfowl at the nation's third oldest zoo.

PREAKNESS BALLOON RACE
   Gala events fill the week before the annual running of the Preakness at Pimlico Race Track. Among the most popular is the colorful Preakness Balloon Race, run from Baltimore across the Chesapeake Bay to the Eastern Shore.

THE BLOCK

The neon marquees of the clubs on Baltimore's infamous Block have featured the names of Blaze Starr, Little Egypt, and many other burlesque queens. Comedians such as Phil Silvers began their careers in clubs like the Two O'Clock Club or The Gayety. The Block has survived public indignation, World Wars, and the onslaught of countless soldiers and fraternities.

P.T. FLAGG'S

The Power Plant now houses P.T. Flagg's, but a century ago the building was the power station for the United Railway and Electric Company. Today, P.T. Flagg's is one of the largest night clubs on the East Coast, and one of the city's most popular night spots.

Fort McHenry National Monument

HISTORIC MONUMENTS

It is no coincidence that in the Baltimore City white pages there is a Monumental Life Insurance Company, a Monumental Uniform Company, Monumental Liquors and Monumental Savings and Loan. For over 150 years, Baltimore has been deservedly called the "Monumental City." Baltimoreans have memorialized everything from our first president to our humblest rowhouses in a monument or museum of one sort or another.

The first and still the most significant of these memorials is the Washington Monument, the shadow of which has made the daily round of Mount Vernon Place since its completion in 1829. Colonel John Eager Howard donated the site in "Howard's Woods" with a noble panorama of the city spread beneath it. It was so distant from town, city fathers concluded, that should the monument topple it would do little damage. On July 4, 1815, while "Professor" Bunzie's band played "Yankee Doodle," the artillery fired a one-hundred gun salute and the Most Worshipful Master of the Baltimore Masons laid the cornerstone. The tall marble column, unembellished yet beautiful in a kind of Doric simplicity, was designed by noted architect Robert Mills.

At nearly the same time a second monument was rising at the corner of Calvert and Lexington Streets. On September 12, 1815, Professor Bunzie was again on hand to herald the commencement of the Battle Monument, in memory of those Baltimoreans who had fallen the previous September when the British forces advanced upon the city.

From the time the two monuments were completed, they were models for the development of the areas around them. Mount Vernon Place has been compared with the finest urban squares in Europe, with its gracious dwellings facing a quiet park filled with the bronzes of Antoine Barye. Battle Monument Square sets a sober example for the lawyers who daily pass, for it is the centerpiece of the city's court and legal community.

Nearly every war in which Baltimoreans have participated has been commemorated in a local monument. A shaft with a female figure on top, at the corner of Cathedral Street and Mount Royal Avenue, recalls the Maryland Line, the state's Revolutionary War unit that was the backbone of Washington's army. The Civil War is also a popular subject for Baltimore sculptors. The Confederate Soldiers' and Sailors' Monument on Mount Royal Avenue is balanced by a similar monument to the armies of the North. Robert E. Lee and Stonewall Jackson are memorialized in Wyman Park and there is a monument to the women of the Confederacy on Charles Street.

Every Baltimore neighborhood has its monument to the fallen in the past two World Wars, and there are assorted statues of Edgar Allan Poe, Johns Hopkins, Mayor Latrobe, Cecilius Calvert, and Francis Scott Key. Among the city's most striking new monuments is the Holocaust Memorial, at Water and Gay Streets, which remembers those who perished in German concentration camps during World War II.

The Francis Scott Key Monument stands on the grounds of the Fort McHenry National Monument and National Shrine. Today, military life of the period is recreated with frequent Tattoos and parades. The restored powder magazine, guardroom, officers' quarters and barracks contain exhibits describing the life of the soldiers who fought here.

Local museums also bear witness to Baltimore's veneration of the past. The Peale Museum, now the centerpiece of the Baltimore City Life Museums, was the first museum in America when it opened in 1814. The Peale is a block from City Hall, and contains a vast collection of Baltimore memorabilia. The second floor of the museum is given over to "Rowhouse," a display that celebrates rowhouse living in Baltimore for three centuries. This imaginative retrospective brings the museum into the realm of day-to-day Baltimore life, for nearly everyone in town has a rowhouse somewhere in his or her past.

At Lombard and Front Streets a collection of museums has grown around the Carroll Mansion, an 1811 townhouse in which Charles Carroll of Carrollton, one of Maryland's signers of the Declaration of Independence, died in 1832. These include The 1840 House, in which the day-to-day life of the family that occupied the humble brick dwelling is portrayed by actors cast in the roles as Irish immigrants. Next door is the Urban Archaeology Museum, with displays illustrating how archaeology aids in unraveling the city's past.

The Maryland Historical Society, near Mount Vernon, is the largest repository of Maryland memorabilia in the state. Its maritime museum memorializes the thousands of Marylanders who have worked the water, and the Darnall Young People's Museum gives children a hands-on historical experience. The period rooms are filled with Maryland furniture, paintings, silver, and decorative arts.

Many other museums keep Baltimore history alive. The Baltimore Industrial Museum displays a turn-of-the-century tailor shop like hundreds that employed immigrant tailors, an oyster-shucking plant and an early printing shop. The B&O Railroad Museum, housed in a century-old roundhouse on the site that is the birth of railroading in America, is an impressive collection of hundreds of locomotives and railroad cars. There's a public works museum, a dental museum, a firefighting museum, a streetcar museum, and even a museum of incandescent light bulbs. The USS Constellation, the oldest ship of the United States Navy, is docked at Harborplace, returning to the city of her birth after over 150 years at sea.

Homes of many famous Baltimoreans are open to the public. The H.L. Mencken House, on Union Square in West Baltimore, memorializes the work of the famous journalist. A tiny home on Amity Street was the residence of Edgar Allan Poe, and the garret in which he worked is furnished as it may have been during the mid-1800's. Another rowhouse, the home of the "Sultan of Swat," one-time Oriole Babe Ruth, contains a baseball museum second in size only to the Baseball Hall of Fame. A simple brick home on Paca Street was the home of Elizabeth Ann Seton, founder of the American parochial school system. Canonized in 1975, Mother Seton was the first American saint.

It's hard to draw the line about what is and what isn't a monument in Baltimore. Every rowhouse in every historic community in an a sense a memorial to the past. The "street arabs" who hawk produce up and down city alleys from horse-drawn wagons, the deck hands who work on the harbor tugs are no less monuments of a sort than are museums or statues. In Baltimore, the past has achieved almost reverential importance, and the city is certainly the better for it.

FORT MCHENRY

On September 13, 1814, Fort McHenry was the final barrier between the British forces in the Baltimore harbor and the embattled residents of the city. The Americans held out throughout a 24-hour bombardment and their courage inspired Francis Scott Key, who observed the attack from a British ship where he was a captive, to pen what would become the National Anthem. Today, a flag flies from a replica of the 1814 flagpole and the rest of the fort's buildings have been restored to their War of 1812 appearance. Uniformed guards reenact life in the fort at the time of the battle.

STAR-SPANGLED BANNER FLAG HOUSE

The flag that Francis Scott Key saw "by the dawn's early light" was made in this humble rowhouse by Mary Pickersgill. The home is authentically restored and furnished in the fashion of the Federal period.

CARROLL MANSION

Charles Carroll of Carrollton was the last surviving signer of the Declaration of Independence when he died in this house in 1832. The building is an excellent example of the home of a wealthy Baltimore merchant in the early 1800's.

BALTIMORE CITY LIFE MUSEUMS

Adjacent to the Carroll Mansion is the Baltimore Urban Archaeology Museum and the 1840 House. In the latter, costumed staff members portray the people who actually lived in the house in 1840, a wheelwright and his family. The archaeology museum explains how the study of unearthed artifacts describes the lives of past generations of Baltimoreans.

MOUNT CLARE

Built between 1754 and 1769, Mount Clare is the only surviving colonial mansion within the Baltimore city limits. It was originally built for Charles Carroll, a Barrister and a cousin of the Declaration of Independence signer of the same name. Mount Clare is furnished as it would have been in the late 1700's, and the gardens and orchards have undergone a recent archaeological study and re-creation. During the Christmas season the mansion is elaborately decorated after the colonial fashion and costumed guides lead guests on candlelight tours.

MARYLAND HISTORICAL SOCIETY

Since its inception in 1844, the Maryland Historical Society has been the most important repository of Maryland memorabilia in the state. The collections include portraits, furniture, silver, clothing, costumes, and an extensive display of maritime artifacts. Part of the collection is housed in the townhouse of philanthropist Enoch Pratt.

BALTIMORE ARTS TOWER

Real Baltimoreans know this as the Bromo Seltzer Tower, for it was here that the popular remedy for indigestion was created. Once it was topped by a 51-foot blue Bromo Seltezer bottle. Today, the tower houses Mayor's Advisory Council on Arts and Culture.

SHOT TOWER

Throughout the 1800's, molten lead was poured from the top this 234-foot tower, falling through sieves and into vats of cold water below. The lead shot went on to become ammunition for hunters and soldiers. A lively recreation of the process, hosted by the "ghost" of an early shotmaker, holds modern visitors spellbound.

The Edgar Allan Poe House

THE POE HOUSE

This tiny rowhouse on Amity Street was the home of the famous writer from 1832 to 1835. He reputedly penned a number of his most famous works from the tiny garret just under the eaves. Poe's final resting place is in Westminster Cemetery, a few blocks away from the house.

THE BABE RUTH BIRTHPLACE AND BALTIMORE ORIOLES MUSEUM

1895 saw the birth of the "Sultan of Swat" in this narrow house in southwest Baltimore. Memorabilia of the Babe's colorful career is displayed along with souvenirs from Orioles history. The Maryland Baseball Hall of Fame, dedicated to every native who has ever played professional baseball, can also be found here.

War Memorial

Peale Museum

Mencken Home

WAR MEMORIAL PLAZA, PEALE MUSEUM

The War Memorial Building, a classic example of Greek Revival architecture, faces the Plaza across from Baltimore's 1867 City Hall. Just a block away is the nation's first museum, the Peale Museum, built in 1814. The Peale family displayed not only their own art here, but everything from mastodon skeletons to the country's first demonstration of gas lighting.

H.L. MENCKEN HOME

The "Bad Boy of Baltimore," journalist and pundit Henry Louis Mencken, lived in this West Baltimore rowhouse from 1883 until his death in 1956. The home, facing restored Union Square Park, looks now as it did when Mencken resided here. The author's study, on the second floor, is a detailed re-creation of the room from which Mencken lambasted politicos, lawyers, actors, and dozens of other public figures during his long career.

BALTIMORE STREETCAR MUSEUM

Time was that Baltimore was crisscrossed with streetcar tracks. But since 1965, when the last streetcar was retired, the Streetcar Museum is the only place in town where one can again ride the trolley. Displays and a film on the history of streetcars take visitors back a century or more.

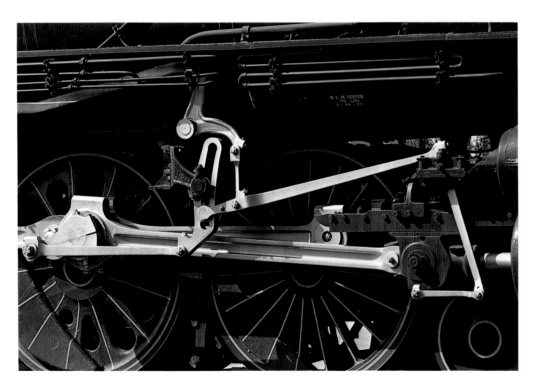

B&O RAILROAD MUSEUM

In an original 1884 roundhouse, the B&O Railroad Museum is an extensive collection of train memorabilia that traces two centuries of railroading history. The museum displays more than 50 cars and locomotives, some restored and others full-size replicas. This is a fitting place for the exhibit, since Baltimore is the birthplace of railroading in America. The country's first passenger depot, Mount Clare Station, has stood here since 1830 and is now part of the museum. Charles Carroll of Carrollton laid the cornerstone for this building and stated it was the second most important thing he had ever done, the most important being his signing of the Declaration of Independence.

Edmondson Village

NEIGHBORHOODS

At first there were but three neighborhoods – Jonestown, Fells Point, and Baltimore Town. What would emerge as the city of Baltimore was the result of the blending of these three as they simply grew together. That single fact, the mingling of three towns into one, set the stage for the social growth of a city that today remains little more than a collection of neighborhoods.

The neighborhood identification is so strong that, were a visitor to Baltimore to ask a resident of Eastern Avenue where he lived, the answer would more likely be Highlandtown than Baltimore. Parish members at St. Leo's think of themselves first as neighbors in Little Italy and second as Baltimoreans. The same goes for those who scrub their white marble steps in Canton, march in the American Day Parade in Locust Point, play pick-up basketball in Harlem Park, toss a lacrosse ball around in Roland Park, and relax on benches in Mount Vernon.

Despite the glitz of the Inner Harbor it is the small neighborhoods that are the real heart of Baltimore, and it is the neighborhoods that give the city its distinctive character. Many are ethnic in nature, usually identifiable by the restaurants that dot the streets – Greek along Eastern Avenue, Chinese on Park Avenue, Italian on Albermarle Street. Even a language, or at least a dialect, "Baltimorese," has grown on neighborhood streets. In Waverly, residents wash dishes in the "zinc" and everyone in "Bawlamer" heads "downyashun" (translation: down the ocean) for vacation.

Other neighborhoods grew up around a market. Union Square is but blocks away from the Hollins Market which preceded it. South Baltimore and Federal Hill houses surround the Cross Street Market, and the Broadway Market is the focal point of Fells Point. Baltimore's market system is unique, a network of open markets in which small businesspeople rent stalls to sell everything from local produce to exotic coffee and tea. In many respects the Baltimore markets have changed little in over two centuries.

In fact, in many Baltimore neighborhoods this resistance to physical change, spawned by an honest respect for the history of the neighborhood, has been the catalyst to drive the area into the future. For some, such as Stirling Street, history has been the incentive to turn around what had become an economic and social downward spiral. In others, like Little Italy, the neighborhood tradition has continued unabated for generations, allowing it to grow and thrive into the twentieth century. Several Baltimore neighborhoods are recognized by inclusion on the National Register of Historic Places and others have become local historic districts. Renovators in these historic neighborhoods are encouraged to return their houses to their early appearance and retain the architectural features which give them their character.

Baltimore neighborhoods have withstood tremendous social pressure in the last thirty years, and yet many survive with much the same temperament as generations ago. The key has been moving into the future with an eye to the neighborhood's past. A combination of contemporary urban revitalization techniques, historic preservation, and simple neighborhood pride has resulted in an urban rebirth unmatched by any city in the United States.

Many locally-grown ideas have spread to other cities. The Urban Homesteading, or "Dollar House," program turned thousands of abandoned houses into modern, comfortable dwellings. Baltimore came to the forefront of American preservation by creating the Commission for Historical and Architectural Preservation in 1964. Other revolutionary home ownership programs,

inventive ways to finance private home buying and restoration, and successful ventures to turn dilapidated commercial buildings into apartments and condominiums have made Baltimore the national leader in neighborhood development.

A strong partnership between residents, the local government, and private business has encouraged change for the better throughout Baltimore. Individual community preservation organizations like the Society for the Preservation of Federal Hill and Fells Point or the Union Square Association have taken active parts in saving important structures, returning their neighborhoods to their past glory and infusing a sense of community pride into residents who have taken on individual home restoration projects. The Citizens Planning and Housing Association has been working for responsible government in the areas of planning, housing, and zoning for more than forty years. Other organizations like the Neighborhood Housing Service have dedicated themselves to helping renters become homeowners, and private industry has joined the effort with innovative programs like Baltimore Gas and Electric's low-cost Home Winterization Program.

For the casual visitor, it may be difficult to penetrate the neighborhood soul of the city. Neighborhoods are distinctly different from each other, often in ways that are clearly visible. The popular painted window screens of East Baltimore, the stately brownstone facades of Mount Vernon, and the pristine garden fronts of Charles Village differentiate one neighborhood from another.

The one thing most neighborhoods have in common is the rowhouse. The humble brick rowhouses of eighteenth century Fells Point are the earliest examples in Baltimore. As the city prospered, its rowhouses became more spacious and elegant, yet they still shared their side walls with their neighbors in long, unbroken rows. Suburban developers have taken to calling them "townhouses," but in Baltimore City there is a sort of a reverse-chic in living in what one proudly calls a rowhouse.

In many respects, one discovers precisely what has made Baltimore a modern, progressive city by visiting the neighborhoods that seem to pass through the ages virtually unchanged. Life here revolves around community activities like church suppers and summer street festivals. People stay in their respective neighborhoods because they like the feeling of identifying with something worthwhile. Increasingly, transplants from surrounding suburbs are returning to inner city neighborhoods because they find something here – a sense of fellowship, perhaps, or the satisfaction that comes from preserving something worth preserving – that is missing in tract house developments and garden apartments.

When out-of-towners talk about the great "Baltimore Renaissance" of the 1970's and 1980's they are usually talking about that part of the city's revitalization most easily observable: the clearing away of rotting piers to create the new Inner Harbor or the proliferation of new restaurants and entertainment centers. The real revitalization of the city, however, is taking place along the streets of its dozens of neighborhoods. Of course, maybe it's not a rebirth at all. Maybe Baltimore has always been a comfortable place to live.

MOUNT VERNON

Long considered Baltimore's most prestigious address, Mount Vernon Place is surrounded by fine brownstone and brick residences. Building here began in the mid-1800's, capitalizing on the white marble Washington Monument that remains the neighborhood's centerpiece. The 1849 Thomas-Jencks-Gladding House and the 1884 Engineering Society (built as a residence for railroad millionaire Robert Garret) are perhaps the finest residences in town. The proud homes face a glade filled with fountains and sculpture, notably the work of French sculptor Antoine Louis Barye. Monumental sculptures of George Peabody, jurist Roger Brooke Taney, and the equestrian statues of John Eager Howard and the Marquis de Lafayette dominate the parks. Peabody Institute and Mount Vernon Place Methodist Church, built in 1872, also face the Square.

MOUNT WASHINGTON

The advent of public transportation made the suburbs around Baltimore attractive residential neighborhoods. Beginning in the 1870's, the city's wealthy flocked to areas like Mount Washington, in the rolling hills overlooking Jones Falls. Many of the Victorian homes still stand, and have been restored to pristine condition. The village of Mount Washington has become a popular shopping area, the old buildings filled with boutiques, antique and gift shops, and galleries.

HAMPDEN

The Jones Falls provided power for several mills that turned out millions of yards of fabric during the 1800's. The millworkers lived in the Hampden-Woodberry neighborhood, in humble brick and stone rowhouses that still cover the hills overlooking the Falls. Mill Center, a community of artists and craftspeople, occupies some of the old mill buildings.

STIRLING STREET

It was called "urban homesteading," but on East Baltimore's Stirling Street it meant rebirth. The famous "dollar house" program was born here, a plan which allowed courageous residents to buy their houses from the city for one dollar. The homes, little more than shells, were then restored to their original appearance by their new owners, sparking private restoration across the city.

Federal Hill

Federal Hill

Seton Hill

Fells Point

FEDERAL HILL, SETON HILL, FELLS POINT

Following a huge celebration in 1788 to mark Maryland's ratification of the United States Constitution, the mound that dominates today's Inner Harbor was named "Federal Hill." Over the years the hill served as a signal tower that advised merchants of the approach of ships, and a fort from which federal forces commanded the unruly city below during the Civil War. Federal Hill is one of Baltimore's first restored neighborhoods, and its streets today are lined with lovely brick homes from the nineteenth century.

Elizabeth Ann Seton, the first American-born saint, lived in a humble brick house on Paca Street in the neighborhood that now bears her name. Seton Hill is characterized by carefully restored narrow rowhouses on equally narrow lanes and alleys.

Fells Point was a booming port of entry when Baltimore was little more than a cow pasture. Some of the old brick warehouses still stand at the water's edge, along with over 200 homes dating back to the mid-1700's. Today, Fells Point is one of Baltimore's most popular nightspots, its streets lined with taverns, restaurants, shops, and galleries.

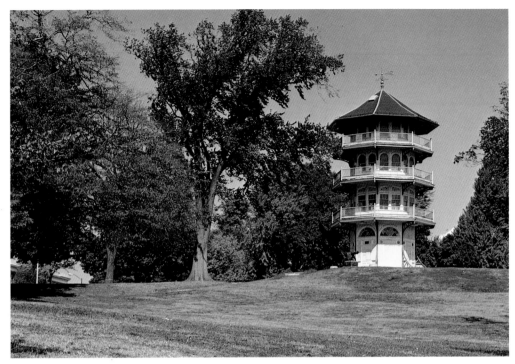

The Pagoda, Patterson Park

Painted window screen, Highlandtown

Baltimore's white marble steps

Northeast Baltimore

EAST BALTIMORE

Baltimore's ethnic showplace, East Baltimore seems to change little from year to year. "The Avenue," Eastern Avenue, is the heart of the community, a bustling retail street with Greek restaurants, taverns, and neighborhood stores. The streets are filled with row after row of brown brick houses, many with well-scrubbed marble steps and the city's only indigenous art form, painted window screens. Patterson Park was the site of the defeat of the British land forces in 1814. Today there are acres of grass, trees, and paths filled with joggers and cyclists, dominated by a four-story "pagoda," built as an observation tower in 1881.

CHARLES VILLAGE

About the turn of the century, when Charles Village was known as Peabody Heights, it was in the northern fringes of Baltimore City. Edwardian rowhouses still line the streets here, most carefully restored by residents who are proud of their neighborhood's unique architecture: their columned parlours, their leaded glass windows, and their ornate oak interior trim. Johns Hopkins University's Homewood campus is nearby, as is the Baltimore Museum of Art and Memorial Stadium, home of the Baltimore Orioles.

BOLTON HILL

One of Baltimore's most elegant neighborhoods, Bolton Hill was the first community in Baltimore to recognize its historical importance and successfully save its fine old rowhouses from the ravages of progress. F. Scott Fitzgerald once called Bolton Hill home, as did Gertrude Stein and the infamous Cone sisters. The rowhouses in Bolton Hill, unlike many other city neighborhoods, have varying facades up and down the same block, creating a patchwork of architectural detail. The Lyric Opera House, Maryland Institute of Art, and Meyerhoff Symphony Hall are nearby.

Roland Park

Dickeyville

Roland Park

Dickeyville

ROLAND PARK

Roland Park has the unique distinction of being one of the first planned communities in the nation. The creator of New York's Central Park, Frederick Law Olmstead, planned the community's extensive landscaping, and the manicured lawns and lovely gardens carry on in this tradition. Houses range from massive frame Victorians to humbler bungalows. The Morgan Millard Restaurant and Gallery, in the country's oldest shopping center, has been a popular neighborhood cafe for nearly eight decades.

DICKEYVILLE

It's hard to remember you're in Baltimore City when in the narrow lanes of Dickeyville. The village was built for mill workers who were employed by the Dickey Company on Gwynns Falls. Dickeyville, with its fine white clapboard homes, ancient trees, and gardens has retained its village ambience.

Union Square

Union Square

West Baltimore

UNION SQUARE, WEST BALTIMORE

A square block of greenery among the bustle of southwest Baltimore, Union Square looks today as it did when it was created in the 1840's. The rowhouses that face the park, built mostly in the years just following the Civil War, have been restored along strict historic guidelines in this neighborhood recognized on the National Register of Historic Places. The H.L. Mencken home is on Union Square, overlooking the original Greek gazebo and the restored fountain.

West Baltimore is rapidly becoming Baltimore's Soho. The area around Hollins Market is a thriving community of local artists, focused on the Market that has stood here for nearly 150 years.

The Walters Art Gallery

THE ARTS

As motorists approach Baltimore, fighting the traffic to Mulberry Street, art is probably secondary to getting to the office on time. Yet here, on the brick wall of a rowhouse where one would least expect, it is a monumental painting. Billboard-like in its scale, it depicts a pair of elderly Baltimoreans hunched over a checkerboard on some city sidewalk. Not only does the painting by Baltimore artist James Voshell capture a bit of Baltimore life, it also sets the stage for the art scene here: expect the unexpected.

For Baltimore is not a city born into the arts. There is no Soho, no enclave where artists from around the world gather to set international trends. Yet don't assume that Baltimore has no foundation of culture. Not only are all aspects of both the visual and the performing arts well represented in Baltimore, but art here saturates life down to street level, or at least just above street level in the case of the many wall paintings like Mr. Voshell's.

In even the most exalted collections there is a special sort of Baltimore link. The Walters Art Gallery, on Mount Vernon Place, has its basis in the collections of merchant William Walters. Walters spent the Civil War in Paris, where he rubbed shoulders with Corot, Daumier, and their counterparts. He began to collect European and Asian art, from paintings to porcelain to Medieval armor. His son Henry continued to expand the collection. Though either the father or the son could easily have moved to major cultural centers like New York or Paris, they chose to keep their artistic wealth here in Baltimore.

The story of one of Baltimore's most important collections, the Cone Collection in the Baltimore Museum of Art, is much the same. The Cone sisters, Claribel and Etta, made some thirty trips to Europe after 1900 where they made friends with Matisse, Picasso and their friends. They began buying the artists' works when no one else was interested in them, works that were little understood in conservative Baltimore.

With its move to the Baltimore Museum of Art in 1949, the Cone Collection testified to the city's artistic awakening, for in her will Claribel had specified that "unless the spirit of appreciation of modern art" showed evidence of growth in Baltimore, the collection should go elsewhere. It stayed in Baltimore, complementing an already-impressive collection of American paintings, period rooms, silver and furniture in the classical Baltimore Museum of Art building. A 1982 addition increased the museum's ability to display its collections, and an outdoor sculpture garden completes the panorama along Art Museum Drive.

The art history of Maryland has its home at the Maryland Historical Society just blocks from Mount Vernon Place. The Society's collection includes portraits of three centuries of prominent Marylanders as well as the enormous Robert G. Merrick collection of Maryland historic prints.

Since its birth in 1826, the Maryland Institute of Art has displayed the work of established artists as well as emerging and student artists. The white marble facade of the main building has been a fixture on Mount Royal Avenue for well over a hundred years. The Institute has aggressively sought other buildings, including the old Mount Royal train station and a defunct shoe factory, converting them to classroom and studio space.

After Charles Center was completed, North Charles Street slowly became the gallery center of Baltimore. A dozen or so private galleries dot the street in the area around Mount Vernon Place, displaying everything from crafts to folk art to contemporary works.

Yet beyond the galleries lies the art of the streets of Baltimore. Just walk down Patterson Park Avenue on a summer day to see Baltimore's most famous indigenous art form: painted window screens depicting cool, mountainous rural scenes. Or take note of the sculptures in front of so many Baltimore schools, part of the city's "1% for Art Program." So much for Baltimore's ancient reputation as a blue-collar, cultural wasteland.

The same can be said for the concert halls and the theatres that play to Baltimore audiences. The Baltimore Symphony Orchestra, whose home is the monumental Joseph Meyerhoff Symphony Hall, has carved a place as a world-class orchestra with concert tours to Europe and the Soviet Union. The Meyerhoff is one of the finest halls in the country, a room so successful that its opening was heralded with a one-hour special on National Public Television simply to describe how it was "tuned" for acoustical perfection.

Since 1895 the Lyric Opera House, home of the Baltimore Opera, has hosted the country's leading virtuosos. The fine old theatre, recently renovated, continues to present not only opera, but ballet and a variety of theatrical performances and cinema. The hall retains the grandeur of the turn of the century, every bit the equal of some of the finest opera houses in Europe.

Mount Vernon Place has become sort of a cultural mecca in Baltimore, largely due to the presence of the Peabody Institute, Baltimore's nationally-recognized conservatory of music. For years the Peabody has been the center of the city's musical life, bringing many of the world's most famous artists here to teach or perform.

Baltimore's Morris A. Mechanic Theatre, which presents Broadway plays and musicals, is rooted in decades of popular musical tradition. Mechanic was the manager of Ford's Theatre when George M. Cohan and Tallulah Bankhead performed there. Lillian Russell, Ethel Barrymore, and Al Jolson appeared in local Vaudeville theatres, and today's Mechanic hosts the country's leading Broadway stars.

Just steps from Mount Vernon Place, Center Stage is the Maryland State Theatre, presenting everything from Shakespeare to Kurt Vonnegut. For over twenty years Center Stage has challenged Baltimoreans with the work of new, talented playwrights and has pioneered updated, daring productions of theatrical classics.

Smaller theatres across Baltimore, including the Arena Stage and a host of repertory companies like the Vagabonds, assure that theatre is accessible to everyone who enjoys the smell of greasepaint. There is a long history of small theatre in the port city, enabling daytime homemakers or accountants to become Juliet, Cyrano, or Willy Loman when the stage lights come up.

But this should be no surprise. Art seems to pervade much of Baltimore life. Ask Baltimore moviemaker John Waters. His popular films often feature the beehive hairdos of East Baltimore and the not-so-lyrical twang of a Highlandtown waitress. Waters finds art everywhere he looks – down narrow city alleys or inside formstone-fronted rowhouses. Maybe Waters is just more perceptive than most Baltimoreans, but in this town of merchant ships and corner taverns one need not look too hard to find Baltimore's particular sort of culture.

THE BALTIMORE MUSEUM OF ART

Situated among the trees of Wyman Park, adjacent to Johns Hopkins University, the Baltimore Museum of Art is home to several important collections. The Cone Collection, which features many works by Matisse, is perhaps the best known. The museum also boasts impressive collections of Maryland furniture and decorative arts, complete room settings salvaged from noteworthy Baltimore homes, and paintings by Cezanne, Picasso, Renoir, and Andy Warhol, among many others. A recently enlarged sculpture garden is nestled among the trees next to the museum.

THE WALTERS ART GALLERY

William Walters made a fortune in the Baltimore mercantile community, and used much of his wealth to amass a huge collection of European and Asian art. He displayed it in his Mount Vernon home, and upon the death of his son Henry, who enlarged the collection, it was presented to the city. The original 1904 gallery has been recently restored and an addition to the museum was built in 1974.

PEABODY CONSERVATORY OF MUSIC

"The Peabody," as most Baltimoreans know this venerable institution, is Baltimore's center of music. Merchant George Peabody created the school in 1866, planning a curriculum that would include the conservatory, a library, a lecture series, and an art gallery.

The library's collection is extensive, and is as impressive as the ornate cast iron balconies which dominate its interior. Today, the Peabody is recognized as one of the finest music conservatories in the nation.

THE MARYLAND INSTITUTE COLLEGE OF ART

In 1826, when the Institute was founded, it became the first college in America dedicated to the study of art. Its Italianate main building, constructed of white marble, has dominated Mount Royal since its opening. The modern school incorporates not only that building, but also a shoe-factory-turned-studio-space, and the old Mount Royal Station, an early train station that has been converted into gallery space, studios, and classrooms.

THE MORRIS MECHANIC THEATRE

Morris A. Mechanic spent years as manager of Baltimore's Ford's Theatre, which had hosted the country's most eminent thespians since 1871. In 1964, when the venerable old building was razed, the modern theatre that would bear Mr. Mechanic's name was begun. Those who have crossed the stage at the Mechanic since then include Katherine Hepburn, James Earl Jones, Rex Harrison, Claudette Colbert, Dustin Hoffman, and dozens of other celebrated actors. The Mechanic presents plays and musicals that are both Broadway veterans and Broadway-bound.

JOSEPH MEYERHOFF SYMPHONY HALL, BALTIMORE SYMPHONY ORCHESTRA

Concertgoers are usually amazed by the hall before the music even begins in Baltimore's Meyerhoff Symphony Hall. The $10.5 million hall, built using state-of-the-art acoustical design, is as perfectly planned and constructed as any concert hall in the country. The sweeping white walls, gracefully curving boxes, and space-age acoustical deflectors take one's breath away. The Meyerhoff is home to the Baltimore Symphony Orchestra, a world class orchestra that has been greeted enthusiastically in concert halls in both Europe and the Soviet Union as well as at home.

Johns Hopkins University, Homewood Campus

COLLEGES & UNIVERSITIES

Baltimore has often been perceived as strictly a working-class town. Yet among Baltimore's institutions of higher learning are one of the country's first medical schools, a nationally recognized music conservatory, and one of the most respected centers of medical research in the world.

Beginning in 1807, with the founding of the University of Maryland, the city has been a regional educational focal point. The history of the University is a litany of educational firsts. The medical school was the first to build a hospital for clinical instruction. A century and a half later, the establishment of the Shock Trauma Unit pioneered research in the treatment of accident-related trauma. Other leading research and patient care specialties at the University include the Intensive Care Neo-Natal Center, the Baltimore Cancer Research Program, and the National Institute for Sudden Infant Death Syndrome.

Today's University of Maryland at Baltimore (the home campus is now in College Park, about thirty miles southwest of Baltimore) also prepares students for careers in the law, social work, nursing and dentistry. The dental school, when it opened in 1840, was the first institutional center of dental education in the world.

The University's second largest campus, University of Maryland Baltimore County, is outside the city in the western suburbs. With nearly 9,300 students, the Baltimore County Campus is a leader in Arts and Sciences education. Its theater department is especially noteworthy, and the library boasts a growing collection of local photography.

Philanthropists have played a major role in the development of higher education in Baltimore. Johns Hopkins grew up on a large farm in Anne Arundel County. He moved to Baltimore in 1813 to work for his uncle Gerard, a commission merchant and grocery distributor, and later made a fortune bottling whiskey. Investments in the port and the B&O Railroad made Hopkins one of the wealthiest men in the country. His will left eight million dollars for the establishment of the university and the hospital that bear his name.

Shortly after the turn of the century, Johns Hopkins University moved from downtown Baltimore to the Homewood campus, north of town. The site had descended from the family of Charles Carroll of Carrollton, and the magnificent Georgian home on the hillside, Homewood, belonged to one of Carroll's children. The modern campus, a blend of conservative classical buildings and contemporary structures, is a fitting home for Baltimore's internationally-known university. Today Johns Hopkins is a world-recognized medical training and research center.

George Peabody, whose million-dollar gift in 1859 established the Peabody Institute, was a native of Massachusetts. Like his compatriots, he earned a substantial fortune in Baltimore's mercantile exchanges and investment banks. His gift provided for "a library, a course of lectures, an academy of music, a gallery of art, and prizes to encourage private and public school pupils."

Peabody Institute eventually became the center of music in Baltimore. The core of the modern program is, of course, classical studies, and there is an impressive library. Also, the Peabody Jazz and Ragtime Ensembles have been known to make generations of Baltimoreans tap their toes. Its department of electronic music was among the first in the country to turn serious attention to what is now known as computer music.

The name Goucher is prominent in the history of education in Baltimore. Goucher College, now in Towson north of Baltimore, was incorporated in 1885 as the Women's College of Baltimore. The first president, Dr. John Goucher, donated the site for the main building on North Charles Street.

Dr. Goucher had already given land and an endowment to the Methodist Conferences of Baltimore for the buildings of the Centenary Bible Institute, now Morgan State University. In 1890 the school began to confer general degrees and the name changed to Morgan College, named for an early member of the Board of Trustees and important donor. Morgan's department of urban planning is recognized as a leader in the field and the school has long been a bastion of black cultural arts.

Another school established to train Baltimore's black youth opened its doors in 1900 as the Colored Training School, with a curriculum dedicated to training teachers. It was renamed the Fannie Jackson Coppin Normal School, after a former slave who was the first black woman in America to earn a college degree. Today's Coppin State College offers a full undergraduate liberal arts curriculum from its west Baltimore campus.

Many Baltimore colleges have religious sponsorship. In 1848 the Sisters of Notre Dame established a boarding school, and in 1873 the land for the college's Charles Street campus was purchased. By 1899 Notre Dame was conferring college-level degrees, and does so still. Neighboring Loyola College began instruction in 1852 with a faculty of eight Jesuits, conducting classes from two houses on Holliday Street. Loyola now offers both undergraduate and graduate curriculums and has been a leader in business education in Baltimore. Countless local executives boast a Loyola MBA on their resumes.

Two-year schools complement the efforts of these colleges. The Community College of Baltimore is one of the first of its kind. CCB has, since its inception in 1947, offered courses that are directed specifically to the needs of the community. Its Center for English as a Second Language was established to help foreign students, and the Liberty Campus Child Development Center addresses the needs of urban pre-school education.

The University of Baltimore, created as a four-year college and eventually becoming a leading local law school, now offers only junior and senior level classes at its Mount Royal Avenue campus. The popularity of community colleges, all of which confer a two-year Associate of Arts degrees, made it apparent that a school which would meet the needs of the community college students was needed.

Towson State University has its roots in Baltimore and has since developed into one of the largest campuses in the Baltimore area. Eleven students enrolled in what was originally strictly a teachers' college, the Maryland State Normal School, when it first operated from North Paca Street in 1869. By 1915 the campus had settled at its permanent location in what was rural Towson. Today it is Towson State University, and though many of its 15,000 students are destined to teach, the university offers a full range of liberal arts curriculums.

One of Baltimore's strengths has always been, and continues to be, the quality of its educational resources. This fact does not go unnoticed in the business community, where new technology companies take advantage of the work done at research centers like the Space Telescope Science Institute at JHU or the University of Maryland Foundation's Research Park, now under development. The park will facilitate interaction between the university's faculty, its research efforts, and the business community.

The contributions of the city's educational institutions have always exceeded what could be expected from a city of Baltimore's size, and the dedication of the city's educators, coupled with the efforts of government and business, will assure Baltimore a prominent place in education and research for years to come.

JOHNS HOPKINS UNIVERSITY

Johns Hopkins University was founded in 1876; since its early days its name has been recognized around the world. The University is a leader in medical research and education, and its contributions in these fields have made its hometown famous. The Homewood campus is arranged around the Carroll family home of the same name; there are also campuses at the Johns Hopkins Hospital in East Baltimore, in downtown Baltimore, and in Washington, D.C.

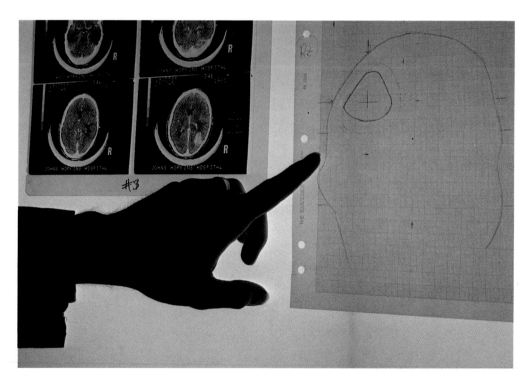

JOHNS HOPKINS HOSPITAL

Opening in 1889 on a Broadway site selected by Hopkins himself, the hospital and the ensuing school of medicine have revolutionized medical training and research. Hopkins continues to be one of the country's most respected institutions, drawing both patients and practitioners from around the world.

Shock Trauma

Sheppard Pratt

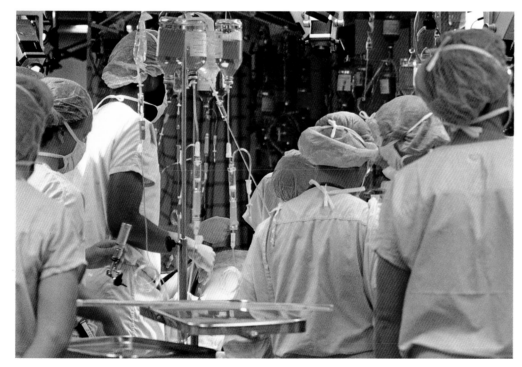

Shock Trauma

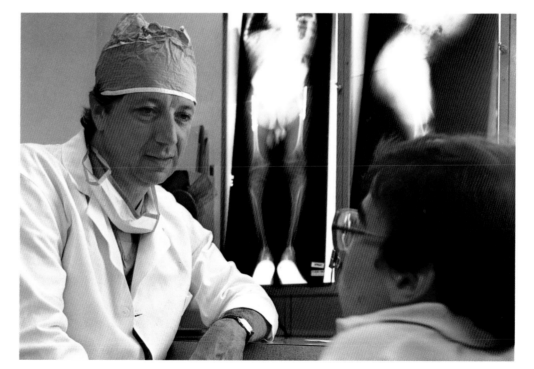

Children's Hospital

MARYLAND INSTITUTE OF EMERGENCY MEDICAL SERVICE SYSTEMS, SHEPPARD PRATT HOSPITAL, CHILDREN'S HOSPITAL

The shock trauma center of the Maryland Institute of Emergency Medical Service Systems (MIEMSS), is located at the University of Maryland Hospital. The center is a national pioneer in the treatment of accident-related trauma, and is known around the world for the development of emergency procedures.

The Sheppard and Enoch Pratt Hospital was one of the oountry's first progressive centers for the treatment of psychiatric disorders. Sheppard Pratt is surely one of the most beautiful medical institutions in Baltimore, located on several rolling hills in Towson.

Children's Hospital is renowned for the treatment of physical deformities and orthopedic problems in children.

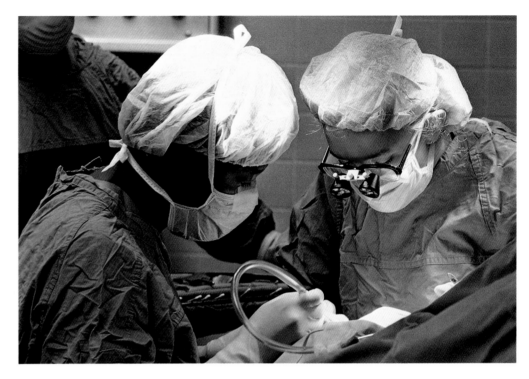

THE UNIVERSITY OF MARYLAND AT BALTIMORE

Founded as a private medical school in 1807, UMAB has remained a leading medical educational institution. The University pioneered the use of a hospital as a teaching clinic, created one of the country's most successful shock trauma centers, and has led the country in research in Sudden Infant Death Syndrome and neo-natal care.

University Of Baltimore

Loyola College

University Of Baltimore

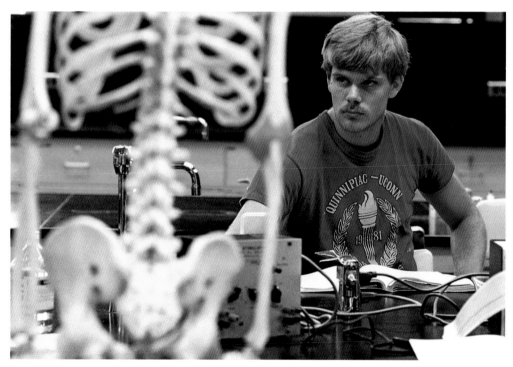

Loyola College

UNIVERSITY OF BALTIMORE

The University of Baltimore, founded in 1925, offers pragmatic programs that prepare students for careers in the government, business, and non-profit sectors of the community. The school became a public institution in 1975, and is now a well-known law school.

LOYOLA COLLEGE

In 1852, Father John Early founded what would become Loyola College in Maryland. Since moving to the North Charles Street campus in 1922, Loyola has established a reputation for excellence in liberal arts. The school's Masters of Business Administration program is Baltimore's most respected graduate business school.

MORGAN STATE UNIVERSITY

Morgan State has a heritage of extending educational opportunities to black students in Baltimore. Founded as the Centenary Bible Institute, Morgan has expanded its program to include a full range of liberal arts degrees. The campus is one of Baltimore's most beautiful, dotted with classic stone buildings.

Towson State University

Towson State University

Goucher College

TOWSON STATE UNIVERSITY

Originally Maryland State Normal School, Towson State University obtained its current status in 1976. Founded as a teachers' college, Towson State now offers over 40 undergraduate degrees and a wide variety of master's degree programs. The school's curriculum is constantly expanding to meet the growing needs of its students.

GOUCHER COLLEGE

Goucher only recently became a co-educational institution, after a century as a women's college. The school was named after Dr. John Goucher, a prominent Baltimore educator in the waning years of the nineteenth century. In 1953, Goucher moved from cramped downtown quarters to the new campus just north of Towson.

The Baltimore Orioles

SPORTS

Baltimoreans take their sports so seriously that they're not content to just do what everyone in Pittsburgh, Dallas, or Los Angeles does. Take duckpin bowling for example. The duckpin bowling capital of the civilized world is undoubtedly Highlandtown-Canton-Dundalk. Here, bowlers roll balls about the size of grapefruit at pins shaped roughly like long neck Coca-Cola bottles. There are no finger holes in the balls.

Some said that the game, with its reduced size balls and pins, was called duckpins because the pins looked a little like wooden decoys. Others claimed it was because they scattered like wild ducks after a volley of buckshot when they were hit. Whatever the reason, this sport original to Baltimore was for a time popular from Maine to Georgia. Today tenpin bowling has returned, but duckpins are still the favorite targets in many east Baltimore lanes.

Lacrosse is another sport that is played in few places except Baltimore. Visitors from Kansas City often cannot figure out why a bunch of boys run up and down the field at Johns Hopkins University waving wooden sticks with little leather nets sewn into one end. Lacrosse is the Canadian national sport, but when it took root in Baltimore in the 1870's no one south of the St. Lawrence River had ever seen it played.

Mount Washington, in North Baltimore, has always been the mecca of American lacrosse. The Baltimore Athletic Club fielded the first American team in a sport which began as a blueblood, high society game and has pretty much continued as such. In New York state the moneyed class plays polo, here they toss around a rock-hard lacrosse ball. The sport has gained in popularity in recent years and is played in prestigious schools like Hopkins, Andover, and Exeter. Ivy League schools play lacrosse with hard-nosed finesse, but this strange sport, which even today is more Indian than American, saw its first U.S. games played in Baltimore.

Professional, nationally-recognized sports have plenty of followers here too. Horse-racing has an honored place in Baltimore history and many famous thoroughbreds have called the hills around Baltimore home. Before the Revolution, John Eager Howard hosted horse races on a piece of property he owned near the present site of Lexington Market. It was not until 1870 that racing in Maryland became an official institution when a tract of land near Baltimore was purchased and Pimlico Race Track was built, and the Maryland Jockey Club was founded.

The 1870 race inaugurated modern racing in the state. That first meet was called the Dinner Party Stakes and was won by a horse named Preakness. In 1873 a race for three-year-olds was added to the schedule and was named for the horse that won that first Dinner Party Stakes.

So the eyes of the nation's racing community are on Baltimore in May of each year when the Preakness, the second race in the Triple Crown, is run at Pimlico Race Track. The other tiers in the Triple Crown are the Kentucky Derby and the Belmont Stakes: the three constitute racing's most hallowed events.

Baltimore's Preakness is more than just a horse race, the week before the running is designated "Preakness Week." The occasion is celebrated by concerts and parties, and is capped off with the annual Preakness Balloon Race, a hot air balloon contest that starts in one of Baltimore's public parks. Before the big event the horses parade past the grandstand, their jockeys wearing the colors of the country's greatest stables. In less than two minutes the great race is over, and the winner is crowned with a horseshoe of Black-eyed Susans. Baltimore's greatest party week also ends, at least until next year.

Racing continues year-round at tracks scattered around the Baltimore area, and in the spring and summer another horseback sport is played on fields in the countryside surrounding the city. Jousting is the Maryland State Sport, and although the knights and ladies tilt at little brass rings rather than each other, the sport retains all its ancient pomp and circumstance.

A series of goalpost-like frames is set up on a track through an open field, and from each a metal ring hangs from a single string. The rider charges along the entire route, skewering rings as he rides; ideally each ring is on the end of his lance as he crosses the finish line. Don't minimize the skill required to spear a ring as small as a half an inch in diameter from the back of a charging horse. There's no armor, of course, but the waving pennants and medieval atmosphere make jousting a unique and exciting sport.

From April to October thousands of Baltimoreans flock to Memorial Stadium when the Orioles are in town. Baltimore brewer Harry Vanderhorst established the first Orioles team in 1880, ostensibly for the purpose of having a ball park in which to sell beer. In 1894, 1895 and 1896 the Orioles won the National League pennant. Those first Birds adopted every tactic imaginable to win, sporting or otherwise. The Orioles were accused of planting extra baseballs in the deep outfield grass and of grabbing baserunners by the belt when they rounded third (there was only one umpire in those days).

For many years after the turn of the century the Orioles were a minor league club. Many of their alumni made their way to the big leagues, however. Slugger George Herman "Babe" Ruth, a native Baltimorean, learned to play the game here, and went on to become the most famous ballplayer of all time. In 1954 big league baseball returned to Baltimore when a group of Baltimoreans purchased the St. Louis Browns and moved them east.

The modern Orioles have one of the winningest records in baseball, with three world's championships under their belts. Memorial Stadium succeeded several old Oriole Parks to become the "O's" home, where millions of fans have watched hall-of-famers like Brooks and Frank Robinson turn miracles on the diamond.

The Baltimore Arena is home to the Skipjacks of the American Hockey League and the Baltimore Blast, the town's representative in the Major Indoor Soccer League. Baltimore is a city of fanatic sports lovers, something that is painfully obvious to any visitor who sits next to a fan who jumps up and screams his brains out every time the Blast scores, a Skipjack puts the puck in the goal or an Oriole drives one over the right field wall.

The new Inner Harbor has brought recreational boating to Baltimore, and now sleek power yachts and graceful sailboats tie up where tugs and steamboats anchored just a few years ago. New marinas stretch along the harbor as far east as Canton. Boaters whose stern boards announce their homes as Fort Lauderdale, Newport, and other yachting capitals regularly call at Baltimore's Inner Harbor.

Baltimoreans love all sorts of sports. In fact, sport in Baltimore is so diverse that one could reasonably expect to find a professional curling team here. Baltimoreans haven't figured out how to host downhill skiing yet, but if Charles Street from the Washington Monument to the harbor were only a bit steeper, you can be sure they'd line the avenue with snow machines.

THE BALTIMORE ORIOLES

Since the Orioles returned to the big leagues in 1954, their home has been Memorial Stadium. The "O's" carry on a long winning tradition of professional baseball in Baltimore, a tradition built on the accomplishments of ballplayers like Babe Ruth, Brooks Robinson, John McGraw, and modern stars Eddie Murray and Cal Ripken. Baltimore fans have an equally-deserved reputation as the finest fans in baseball, avidly supporting the team through its long years of development and into the glory years of American League Pennants and World Championships. A new stadium in the old Camden railway yards near the Inner Harbor may be open for the 1991 season.

THE BALTIMORE SKIPJACKS

Not long after the opening of the Baltimore Civic Center, now the Baltimore Arena, professional ice hockey came to Baltimore. The "Jacks" have always been determined competitors in this sport, noted for its hard checking and fast pace. Baltimore fans quickly discovered the Canadian game, and fill the stands whenever the Jacks are in town.

THE BALTIMORE BLAST

Indoor soccer is the newest professional sport in Baltimore, and its action and fast pace spawned an instant following. The team won the Major Indoor Soccer League championship not long after its creation and also holds the league record for most sell-outs in a single season.

PIMLICO RACE TRACK

Maryland's first horse-racing association was formed in Baltimore in 1823. This fledgling club eventually became the Maryland Jockey Club, but it was not until 1870, under the impetus of Governor Oden Bowie, that racing achieved formal recognition in the state. Since then, Pimlico Race Track has been the unofficial home of thoroughbred horse racing in Maryland. Every year in May the second jewel in racing's Triple Crown, the Preakness, is run here.

LACROSSE

Baltimore's first game of lacrosse was probably played on September 20, 1878. The sport, transplanted from New England where it was first played by the Indians, was immediately popular in local prep schools and private clubs. Johns Hopkins University, the University of Maryland, and the U.S. Naval Academy in Annapolis are dominant academic forces in the sport.

THE MARYLAND HUNT CUP

Held during the steeplechase season, the Hunt Cup is one of the state's most popular spectator events. This event is considered one of the most challenging courses in the country, requiring skill and great coordination between horse and rider. The course is comprised of 22 jumps in a four-mile circuit through the rolling hills of Baltimore County. Some of the jumps have taken their toll; one has been dubbed the "Union Memorial," no doubt after the local hospital of that name.

PLEASURE BOATING

As marinas begin to encircle Baltimore Harbor, the tugs and freighters that have called on the city for centuries are forced to share the water with a growing number of recreational boaters. The harbor gives boaters easy access to the broad Chesapeake Bay, and most weekends of the year find the waters busy with sailboats and power boats. The Baltimore Rowing Club, whose members can be seen powering the slim, fast rowing shells in the Patapsco River, has an impressive clubhouse on a shoreline that was recently little more than a graveyard for abandoned vessels.

The Port of Baltimore

THE PORT

When the first settlers in Baltimore set up shop along the banks of the Patapsco in the early 1700's, it was the potential port which drew them to the spot. They recognized its easy access to the Chesapeake Bay, its vast protective harbor, the prosperity of nearby agricultural sectors in neighboring colonies, and its proximity to the already-flourishing waterfront villages of Fells Point and Jonestown.

What they could not have imagined was the role the Port of Baltimore would play in international affairs in coming centuries, largely due to attributes of the port they could not have known. As the American hinterland developed it happened that Baltimore was the harbor closest to the burgeoning West by virtue of its inland location. As manufacturing centers like Pittsburgh emerged from the mountainous wilderness, the benefits of shipping into and out of Baltimore were magnified.

This prime location was the impetus for the early development of the American railroad system, with Baltimore as its heart and soul. Trains strengthened the link between the Maryland city and the factories westward, and the Port of Baltimore became a railroad port.

By 1812, *Niles Weekly Register* could report that the city had attained "a degree of commercial importance which has brought down upon it the envy and jealousy of all the great cities in the Union." The War of 1812 boosted shipbuilding and sent Baltimore Clippers to ports throughout the western world. The resources developed meshed nicely with the railroad, which began to dominate the port by the Civil War. While that war devastated trade in general, Baltimore emerged stronger than ever, expanding its trade as the rails crisscrossed the country.

Small Chesapeake Bay boats called here, filled with produce from the Eastern shore in the summer and oysters in the fall and winter. Larger schooners, huge vessels carrying as many as five tall masts, ferried lumber from Baltimore to South America and the West Indies, returning with copra or dyes destined for the aniline works along Boston Street.

Baltimore's access to growing points inland was secured by the railroad, canals, and other modes of transportation. The first major dredging of the channel came in 1892, allowing several new terminals to be built just after the turn of the century. By 1920, Baltimore was a port of call for thirty-none overseas steamship lines, thirteen coastal companies, and nine intercoastal shipping lines.

Passenger travel was also a large part of the life of the port until just after World War II. The Old Bay Line steamers, among others, served all parts of the Chesapeake region, and many Baltimoreans looked forward to a leisurely cruise from Baltimore to Richmond, Norfolk, or north to Head of Elk with connections to Philadelphia. The era closed with several boats operating from the harbor near today's Harborplace to resorts on the Eastern Shore like Tolchester and Betterton.

With the demise of the paddlewheeler came other changes that would threaten Baltimore's dominance of Middle Atlantic shipping. In the early 1970's the port was still handling record volumes of cargo, dependent on four commodities: oil, grain, coal, and iron ore. Ships from Baltimore were bound to ports like Calcutta and Saõ Paulo. These third world labor forces had begun to compete with traditional Baltimore industries like shoemaking and clothing manufacturing, and soon the city was importing consumer goods from these points as well as Taiwan, Hong Kong, and other Far East centers of newly-emerging economic strength.

Shipbuilding was still an important port activity through the early postwar years. The first container ships were built here in 1954 and the first jumbo oil tankers shortly thereafter. Freighters increased in size tenfold in just a decade, necessitating a deepening of the channel as well as adjustment of all land-based port facilities. Cranes were installed at the Dundalk Marine Terminal to handle the new container tonnage. A mechanized iron ore pier was built in Sparrows Point and a jungle of cement silos grew in Curtis Bay to accommodate the massive maws of the new ships.

But at the same time the port found itself still shackled to the railroad interests that owned much of the commercial waterfront, particularly within the Baltimore city limits. The railroad industry was moribund and capital-poor, paying little in taxes while controlling the most valuable industrial development land in Baltimore.

It was clear as early as 1950 that a controlling authority would have to be established to coordinate the needed development. In 1956 the Maryland Port Authority was created, and in 1971 it became the Maryland Port Administration.

Today's port serves the trading needs of a number of partners, notably in Europe and Asia. The port's two largest import trade partners are Japan and West Germany. The major trading partner in terms of tonnage is nearby Canada. The export trade, both measured in dollars and tons, is smaller than the imports, and once again Japan and West Germany are the two main partners.

Coal and grain are still the leading commodities to pass through the port on the export side. Food products make up about a tenth of the exported material that passes down the Chesapeake from Baltimore's waterfront. On the import side, raw materials such as lumber, minerals and rubber still dominate trade in Baltimore, though automobiles have become an important new source of import tonnage.

Through the combined efforts of private trading companies and the Maryland Port Administration, the competitive advantages of the Port of Baltimore are marketed on an international basis. As a result, new markets are opening, merchandise arriving at a growing rate from South America and Europe. Deeper access channels are being dredged to accommodate modern ships, and improvements in existing facilities will assure that the port enters the twenty-first century with adequate incentives to attract cargo.

The slogan of the Maryland Port Administration is "We Make It Work," a promise that is based on the port's dedication to providing the best service on the East Coast. That devotion to continuing the port's tradition of success, coupled with a zealous drive to modernization will keep Baltimore among the world's leaders in international trade.

THE PORT OF BALTIMORE

This modern port hosts vessels from many trading partners, mostly from Europe and Asia. Through the combined efforts of the private sector and the Maryland Port Administration, the benefits of shipping into Baltimore are marketed internationally. Deeper channels are being dredged to give larger, more efficient access to the port.

CURTIS BAY TOWING COMPANY

Founded in 1910, the Curtis Bay Towing Company now offers tugboat services in three cities, including its Baltimore headquarters. Tugs accompany and dock ships carrying coal and grain, as well as imported automobiles, steel, and lumber products. Curtis Bay made history when it docked the *Queen Elizabeth II* during its first visit to Baltimore in 1986.

DUNDALK MARINE TERMINAL

In 1982, the final berth was constructed at the Dundalk Marine Terminal, Baltimore's most modern port facility. The largest berth at Dundalk can handle some of the largest container ships afloat, with two 40-ton cranes that lift multi-ton containers easily. Support facilities at the terminal include 25 public warehouses with over 6 million square feet of enclosed storage space and nearly 5 million cubic feet of cold storage. There is extensive office space for shipping firms, customs house clearing agencies, and stevedoring services. The terminal also transfers tens of thousands of imported automobiles annually, with complete facilities that prepare the cars for delivery to their new owners.

FRANCIS SCOTT KEY BRIDGE

This single-span bridge crosses Baltimore's harbor as one of the city's many modern transportation routes. Highways ringing the city give Baltimore businesses easy access to New England, the Ohio Valley, and growing markets to the south. Other links in the transportation network include the Port, an extensive rail system, and a modern airport.

BALTIMORE-WASHINGTON INTERNATIONAL AIRPORT

Over 300 flights depart daily from BWI to domestic and international destinations. Many Baltimoreans still fondly call the airport "Friendship," its name before its routes began to span the globe. Although BWI serves over 25 domestic airlines and a growing air freight business, it is still a manageable airport. Its unique design gives passengers easy access to dozens of gates, without the confusion and multiple terminals characteristic of other American airports.

Bethlehem Steel Corporation, Sparrows Point

ECONOMIC OVERVIEW

Business in Baltimore, like nearly everything else, is a harmonious blend of both old and new. The port city is blessed with a two-century-old tradition of mercantilism. Throughout the post-war years the commerce has stayed, but the products have changed. Still, should merchant-banker Alexander Brown return from his grave of 150 years, or should railroadman John Garrett or businessman Johns Hopkins choose to do the same, they would probably fit comfortably into the Baltimore business community with little adjustment.

Historically the Port of Baltimore has served as the cornerstone of the city's economy and will continue to be a respected world-class port well into the twenty-first century. The existence of the port created an infrastructure that has supported local business since the very earliest days – banking, brokerage activities, related transportation and communications, insurance and risk management, and manufacturing. A strong economic foundation has helped nurture new business here, and as the face of commerce changes the same commercial assets have simply changed gears to back emerging companies in high technology and financial services, education and tourism.

In 1986, a survey of 322 economic development officials conducted by the National League of Cities chose Baltimore for its top honors, praising the city's waterfront development and its revitalized downtown. In fact, the new direction for the city includes a lot more than just sprucing up some neighborhoods and planting some romantic eateries and glitzy shops along the harborfront. Baltimore's renaissance cuts deeply through the business sector in recognition of the fact that industry, like everything else here, needed to adapt to change or perish.

Much of this transition is yet to unfold, but Baltimore has clearly become a leading regional financial center and an important area of technological development, largely due to the insight of its business and government leaders and a resolve by both parties to work in concert toward the agreed-upon ends. The city is slowly shedding its blue-collar image as the focus of its manufacturing changes. While the economy has suffered from the decline of some old-line local manufacturers, and while the extent of these dramatic changes is still yet to be understood, leaders have responded rapidly and decisively to meet the new challenges.

Many old affiliations remain, stronger than ever. Products with labels like Noxzema, Chevrolet, McCormick Spice, London Fog, and Black and Decker, names associated with Baltimore for decades, still leave the port city for destinations scattered around the globe. Services offered by Baltimore firms like United States Fidelity and Guaranty, Maryland Casualty Company, or any of the countless banking houses headquartered here continue to have an impact on the global business sector. More and more, however, they are being complemented by organizations new to Baltimore – Control Data Corporation, Space Telescope Science Institute – that are doing business in the new frontiers of technology. Other Baltimore companies like Westinghouse Electric Corporation and Martin-Marietta Corporation were high-tech before "high-tech" became dinner table conversation.

The growth and change had its inception in the late 1950's with the creation of the Greater Baltimore Committee, a group comprised of area business leaders who wanted to insure that the city didn't slip into economic backwaters. The committee's first major project was the development of Charles Center. Ground was broken in 1961 for the development which, it was hoped, would halt the deterioration in the downtown business district and breathe new life into the city's cultural and economic heart. Private business financed major portions of the project along Charles Street, once Baltimore's most fashionable address.

With the completion of One Charles Center and the opening of the Baltimore Civic Center (now the Baltimore Arena) and the Morris Mechanic Theatre, a new spirit of optimism flowed up Charles Street. City leaders felt it was time to consider a master plan that would encompass every aspect of future development in the business community. Out of this Charles Center Inner Harbor Management, Inc. was born, a group that would oversee the implementation of the plan. Other groups grew from CCIH's example. The Market Center Development Corporation's goal is to rejuvenate the Lexington Market-Howard Street retail area, and the impact of the Baltimore Economic Development Corporation (BEDCO) has been phenomenal.

Through BEDCO, the city develops and administers a number of business parks that serve both to keep old Baltimore businesses and to attract new firms to the burgeoning economic environment. Currently, ten business communities fall under BEDCO's umbrella. In addition, BEDCO has participated in a number of joint ventures to encourage the development of new types of business in the city, notably a cooperative effort with Johns Hopkins University to create a biotechnological business and medical research center.

Baltimore serves as the northern boundary of the Baltimore-Washington Common Market, and as such is becoming a center of science and technology. Nearly two thousand companies in electronics, operations research, medical research, environmental subjects, and computer technology are located in the Baltimore-Washington corridor. Telecommunications and data processing related services are well represented in Baltimore as well. Slowly the old Patapsco River city's commercial perspective is changing. Gone are the brick factories, many of the shipyards, the breweries, and the smokestack businesses on which much of the city's strength was traditionally built. In their place are the space-age corporations that will carry the city well into the twenty-first century.

Economic changes go hand-in-hand with the changing face of Baltimore. Just blocks from the Inner Harbor the Baltimore Convention Center has helped bring hundreds of thousand of conventioneers to see Charm City since its opening in 1979. As visitors poured into town the need for new hotels, restaurants, and related tourist activities became apparent. Since the opening of the Convention Center, and the adjoining Festival Hall, over two thousand new hotel rooms have opened. Restaurants have sprung up in all the old dining centers like Little Italy and North Charles Street as well as in nearby Fells Point and South Baltimore, and on every winding alley in the old financial center.

The most tangible result of all these new economic developments is the addition of thousands of new jobs in industries that didn't even exist in Baltimore twenty years ago. Though the city has a long way to go in adjusting to the loss of jobs in the manufacturing sector, cooperation among Baltimore's citizens, business leaders and government and their zealous determination to adapt to the dramatically-changing face of American business will assure Baltimore a prominent place in the world economy for decades to come.

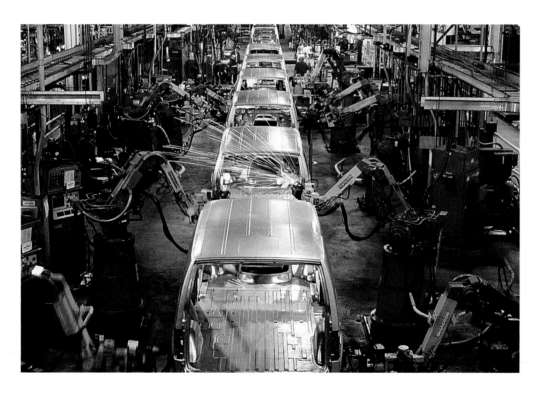

GENERAL MOTORS

The General Motors Truck and Bus Assembly Plant in Baltimore is one of the most modern facilities of its type in the country. Currently employing about 4,000 people, it features state of the art robotics production equipment installed as part of a $300 million modernization program in 1984. The plant produces over 200,000 mid-sized vans annually for the Chevrolet and GMC divisions of General Motors, and will soon produce its 10 millionth vehicle since production began in March, 1935.

THE RYLAND GROUP

Based in Columbia, Maryland, Ryland is known in 17 states coast to coast as one of the largest home builders in the nation. Since 1967, more than 70,000 families have found a home in Ryland. But Ryland boasts a record of building more than homes. The company is also recognized for its strong standing in the mortgage banking and modular home building fields.

AT&T

The cornerstone of AT&T's business is its technological leadership. Its employees are working at the boundaries of science and engineering, quickly bringing the benefits of both to the marketplace. Whether providing high-tech products and services for information movement and management or developing state of the art equipment for the telecommunications network, AT&T is committed to keeping the people of Baltimore in touch with the rest of the world.

BALTIMORE GAS & ELECTRIC COMPANY

The majority of the Baltimore metropolitan region's energy is supplied by Baltimore Gas & Electric Company. One of the most efficient and responsive public utility companies in the nation, BG&E has held down consumer energy costs for services supplied by its system's generating capacity of 5,000,000 kilowatts. Natural gas is supplied to the area through a pipeline connector system which is supplemented by its own synthetic gas generating plant. The nuclear power plant at Calvert Cliffs has supplied more than 50% of BG&E's total service requirements since its opening in 1977; its efficiency has saved customers over 2.8 billion in fuel costs.

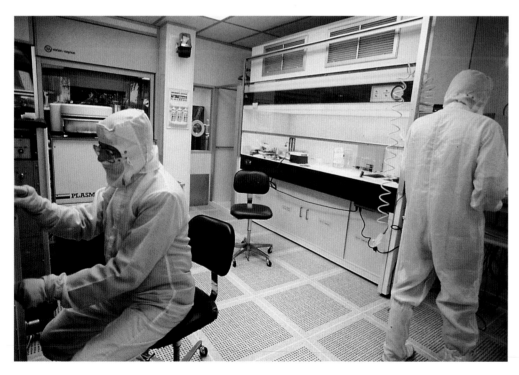

O'CONOR, PIPER AND FLYNN

Since 1984, O'Conor, Piper and Flynn has been the leading locally-owned real estate company in Maryland. With 40 offices specializing in residential, commercial/industrial, and investment real estate, the firm continues to grow, with annual sales of over $1 billion. O'Conor, Piper and Flynn is a full service real estate company, and is recognized for innovative marketing and respected for its hundreds of years of combined industry experience.

MARTIN MARIETTA CORPORATION

An aerospace, electronics, and information technology company, Martin Marietta Corporation's Aero & Naval Systems operation in Middle River features engineering and precision manufacturing technology for defense systems. Martin Marietta Laboratories, in Catonsville, is the corporation's research center. The huge B-26 Marauder bomber once rolled off Martin Marietta's Baltimore assembly lines, but today's technological challenges are found in microelectronic circuits that are smaller than a single particle of dust.

RTKL

Since its beginnings as a two man practice in Annapolis over 4 decades ago, RTKL Associates, Inc. has grown to become one of the nation's largest architecture/engineering firms, with over 500 employees in its Baltimore, Washington, Dallas, Los Angeles, and Fort Lauderdale offices. The distinctive Signet Tower and Bank of Baltimore building are two of RTKL's most recent contributions to Baltimore's evolving skyline.

PEPSI-COLA COMPANY OF BALTIMORE

The Pepsi-Cola Company of Baltimore is an operating unit of PepsiCo Inc., a Fortune 40 company. As a part of the network of company-owned bottling operations located in major markets throughout the country, Pepsi-Cola Company of Baltimore bottles and distributes Pepsi products to the greater Chesapeake area. The company is a major employer in the Baltimore area, and has been an active supporter of the Baltimore community for over 50 years.

CROWN CENTRAL PETROLEUM CORPORATION

One of the largest corporations headquartered in Baltimore, Crown Central Petroleum Corporation is a major distributor of petroleum products in Maryland and other Mid-Atlantic and Southeastern states. Besides numerous clean, efficient retail outlets throughout the area, they also have a major terminal and storage facility in Baltimore. With gross sales in excess of $1 billion, Crown has been ranked in the Fortune 500 listing among the top 300 industrial companies in the United States. The company is a long-time supporter of community activities in the city.

BLACK AND DECKER

Founded in 1910, Black and Decker is the world's leading marketer and manufacturer of power tools and household products. The Towson-based company markets its products in over 100 countries and its sales exceed 2 billion annually. Well known for innovation, quality, and cordless technology, these characteristics extend through its full line of consumer and professional power tools, lawn and garden products, power tool accessories, and household appliances.

FIRST NATIONAL BANK OF MARYLAND

Since First National Bank of Maryland opened its doors as the Mechanics Bank of Baltimore in 1806, it has grown stronger and held firm through Baltimore's history: from economic cycles to the Great Baltimore Fire. Headquartered at 25 South Charles Street, the bank's service area now spans the Chesapeake Bay and Allegheny Mountains.

THE CHESAPEAKE AND POTOMAC TELEPHONE COMPANY

C & P Telephone provides telephone service to more than 700,000 customers throughout the Baltimore metropolitan area. Advanced communications and data transmission systems give C & P a high level of reliability in connecting Baltimore businesses and residents with the rest of the world.

McCORMICK & COMPANY

McCormick and Company is a diversified specialty food company and a world-wide leader in the manufacturing and marketing of seasoning and flavoring products. The company was founded in 1889 and now nets over $1 billion in annual sales.

MICROPROSE SOFTWARE, INC.

Now a world-renowned developer of sophisticated computer games, MicroProse Software began in 1982 in the basement of an energetic former Air Force jet fighter pilot. With his Wharton MBA and can-do attitude, he successfully marketed the work of his partner, an unassuming programming genius with an intuitive flair for game design. MicroProse enjoys an unparalleled reputation for realism, attention to detail, and satisfying game play in simulations of civilian aviation, military technology, and historical adventure. The Hunt Valley firm has offices across the United States and in England, France, Germany, and Japan.

The Chesapeake Bay

SURROUNDING AREAS

Baltimore attorney Peter Carnes constructed a 35-foot balloon out of "beautiful, costly and variegated silks" in the spring of 1784. On June 3, Carnes ascended above Baltimore from Howard Woods, the site of today's Washington Monument. The event was unofficially the first balloon ascension in the United States.

If Carnes had recorded what he saw from above the city he would have written that all roads led to Baltimore. Along Rolling Road he would have seen plantation workers rolling hogsheads of tobacco from Baltimore County to the wharves along the Patapsco. From Ellicott's Mills in Howard County he would have reported wagons of grain slowly moving along Frederick Road into the city. He could not have missed traffic along Philadelphia Road nor could he have ignored the sailing vessels making their way to the harbors of Fells Point and Baltimore Town.

Two hundred years later a similar event takes place annually: the Preakness Balloon Race. The balloon captains could draw much the same conclusion as Carnes. Trucks approach Baltimore from every direction filled with all manner of goods. Ships lie in the harbor waiting to discharge cargo from around the world and fill their holds with ore, cement, or coal. Baltimore has become permanently established as the focal point of the entire region.

To be the economic and cultural heart of a state as diverse as Maryland is quite an accomplishment. More than anything, it is the Chesapeake Bay that defines what Baltimore is and why it has developed as it has. This wide, salty estuary has for generations provided a bountiful harvest for the tables of Baltimoreans and others, and its deep shipping lanes have carried both goods and people into the city.

The state capital in Annapolis is one of the best-preserved colonial cities in America, keeping not only its eighteenth century appearance, but also its southern tradition of hospitality. For nearly three hundred years the state legislature has met here annually in the State House, with its commanding view of the city and the small harbor. Maryland's elected representatives still meet in the same building that hosted Washington, Madison, Jefferson and their contemporaries. The streets of Annapolis are lined with ancient homes; many carefully-restored residences, and others converted to shops and restaurants.

At Solomon's Island, in southern Maryland's Calvert County, the Chesapeake Bay is about nine miles wide. Just across the choppy water is the Eastern Shore (the only region in Maryland whose name, by agreement among residents, should be capitalized). The Bay is more than just a geographic division. As far as Eastern Shore citizens are concerned, it delineates an area which is culturally and socially distinct.

It's hard to deny that they have a point, for almost immediately after crossing the Chesapeake Bay Bridge near Annapolis the feeling of a slower-paced, tradition-bound society descends. Little seems to have changed here, largely because Eastern Shore people have never been in a hurry to adopt "progress." Watermen bristle at the thought of state control over the Chesapeake and its Eastern Shore tributaries, defending their age-old right to freely harvest the Bay's bounty.

To many it appears that the region's single concession to the twentieth century is Ocean City, the state's only Atlantic resort, stretching along miles of sandy beach. "OC" is the destination of tens of thousands of vacationers who head east every weekend from May through September. There's a superb beach, excellent hotels, restaurants and night spots. Nearby Assateague Island is popular among campers, fishermen, amateur naturalists and beach bums.

The middle and upper shores have managed to pass through three centuries virtually unscathed. Easton, the unofficial capital of the area, has kept its small-town personality. Its streets are lined with shops whose windows display Eastern Shore fashion (hunting and sailing garb), carved decoys and waterfowl art.

It is the western shore, particularly the state's broad, fertile central section that extends from the Bay to Pennsylvania to the north and to the foothills of the Appalachians in the west, that is Maryland's economic pulse. Baltimore, of course, provides the infrastructure – the financial institutions, the port, and much of the work force – upon which central Maryland depends. Major industrial parks have sprung up from former farmlands around the Baltimore Beltway. Cattle still graze within sight of a rapidly-growing high technology center near Gaithersburg. The proximity of the nation's capital has attracted all manner of enterprise to the Maryland counties which border Washington, D.C.

To the west, as one enters Frederick County, the Appalachian Mountains begin to rear above the farms. Frederick, a nineteenth century railroad town that is popular for its century-old buildings and its small-town personality, is the gateway to the Maryland mountain playground. Beyond the county's rocky fields the entire character of the state changes. Centuries after the first settlers made their way through the mountain passes to settle in towns like Cumberland and Hagerstown, there's still a pioneering feeling here. Western Marylanders acknowledge the existence of Baltimore, and some will even admit the economic importance of the distant city, but still defend their independence from Baltimore in particular and city-life in general.

Garrett County is as far as one can go from Baltimore and still be in Maryland, and maybe the influence of Baltimore this far west is eclipsed by much-closer Pittsburgh. Yet thousands of Marylanders make Garrett County's green spaces, mountains, and lakes their vacation favorite. Perhaps more than any other resort spot in the state, the western Maryland mountains can claim to have year-round attractions, for they draw fishermen, campers, and sun-seekers in the summer and skiers after the weather turns cold.

For many years Maryland has touted itself as "America in Miniature." Baltimore is the focal point of the diverse state, its economic heart. But this is a two-way street. Without the resources of the lands surrounding the city, and without the easy access from Baltimore to points west, there would be no port on the Patapsco River. Though a waterman on Smith Island or a mountain family in Cresaptown may disagree, the partnership between Baltimore and Maryland has been healthy and mutually beneficial.

ANNAPOLIS

Annapolis has been Maryland's state capital since 1694. The Legislature still meets here, in the same building that has hosted the likes of George Washington, Thomas Jefferson, and James Madison. The Maryland State House, on a gentle hill overlooking the Annapolis harbor, is the oldest building in the nation in continuous use as the seat of local government. In fact, Annapolis has more pre-Revolutionary brick buildings than any other city in the nation. Modern Annapolis is also the home of the United States Naval Academy, founded in 1845. The city is one of the leading ports on the East Coast for sailing yachts, as well as a growing center of tourism.

SOUTHERN MARYLAND

Governor Leonard Calvert arrived in St. Mary's County in 1632 with the first band of English settlers to call Maryland home. This has been tobacco country ever since, its rolling fields filled with low-growing tobacco plants, drying-barns, and tobacco warehouses. Tourists are just discovering Southern Maryland, finding gems like the boating center of Solomons Island, the fossils so easily found along the beach near Calvert Cliffs, and the farmers' market in Charlotte Hall.

North Central

Washington D.C.

CENTRAL MARYLAND

Rolling farmlands surround Baltimore, so rural landscapes and a rural way of life begin not far from the Baltimore Beltway. However, the farmland of Baltimore, Harford, Carroll, and Howard Counties is slowly giving way to modern industrial parks and suburban developments. Just twenty minutes from Harborplace is Columbia, one of the country's earliest and most successful planned cities.

Eastern Shore

Ocean City

WESTERN MARYLAND

The mountains of Western Maryland are the state's only year-round recreation area: skiing in the winter, and hiking, fishing, and camping in the summer. This beautiful section of the Appalachian Mountains includes the Cumberland Gap, gateway to the mid-west for thousands of early settlers.

EASTERN SHORE

For many Baltimoreans, Ocean City *is* the Eastern Shore, but there's much more than just beach and boardwalk in this land of water and fishing villages. Separating the Atlantic Ocean from the Chesapeake Bay, the Eastern Shore offers all manner of outdoor recreational opportunities plus the attractions of sophisticated towns like Easton and Chestertown.